TWENTIETH CENTURY VIEWS

The aim of this series is to present the best in
contemporary critical opinion on major authors,
providing a twentieth century perspective on
their changing status in an era of profound
revaluation.

Maynard Mack, *Series Editor*
Yale University

E D I T H
WHARTON

A COLLECTION OF CRITICAL ESSAYS

Edited by
Irving Howe

A SPECTRUM BOOK

Prentice-Hall, Inc., *Englewood Cliffs, N. J.*

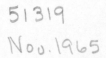

813.52
H83e

51319
Nov. 1965

Third printing ...... June, 1965

© 1962 BY PRENTICE-HALL, INC., ENGLEWOOD CLIFFS, N. J.

LIBRARY OF CONGRESS CATALOG CARD NO.: 63-7990

Printed in the United States of America

95179-C

Table of Contents

EDITH WHARTON

Introduction: The Achievement of Edith Wharton

by Irving Howe

"Justice to Edith Wharton"—this was the title, and the motivating plea, of an essay the distinguished American critic Edmund Wilson wrote soon after Mrs. Wharton's death in 1937. Years have passed; a modest quantity of critical writing about her work has appeared; she still commands the respect of a certain number of readers, just as some, though not enough, of her books are still in print. But if one judges by the treatment she receives in our standard literary histories, the attention given her in the universities, the influence she exerts upon present-day writers, the feelings serious literary people are likely to have about their faded memories of her novels—then justice has not yet come to Edith Wharton. And this seems particularly true if one believes her to be a writer of wit, force and maturity—not the peer of Hawthorne, Melville and James, but several strides ahead of many twentieth century novelists who have received far more praise than she has.

The amount of first-rate criticism devoted to Mrs. Wharton's novels is small, and I doubt that in editing this collection I have omitted many essays that would add significantly to our understanding of her art. Even two or three of those that follow are somewhat lukewarm in their appreciation, as if it were not good form to claim for Mrs. Wharton the distinction she truly possessed. At the moment, however, what matters is that the critical issues posed by her work should again be raised, so that she may take her rightful place as a living figure in the literary world.

In writing this introduction I have chosen not to compose still another formal essay, but instead to present a few critical notes

1

that will isolate the problems faced by Mrs. Wharton's critics. I have borrowed from and where it seemed necessary, even quarreled with the contributors to this book, all in the conviction that Mrs. Wharton, if not a great writer, is a genuinely distinguished one.

The Range of Her Achievement. It is difficult to imagine a study of Mrs. Wharton's apprentice fiction in which sooner or later the word "clever" failed to appear. I quote a few characteristic sentences from her early stories:

> The most fascinating female is apt to be encumbered with luggage and scruples.

> Her body had been privileged to outstrip her mind, and the two . . . were destined to travel through an eternity of girlishness.

> His marriage had been a failure, but he had preserved toward his wife the exact fidelity of act that is sometimes supposed to excuse any divagation of feeling; so that, for years, the tie between them had consisted mainly in his abstaining from making love to other women.

Such writing yields pleasure of a kind, but in the context of Mrs. Wharton's early stories it often seems willful and strained. One senses too quickly the effort behind the cleverness, the claw inside the glove. (Dealing with personal relationships among the leisured and cultivated classes, these stories are usually brittle and contrived, reflections of the conflict in Mrs. Wharton between a worldliness that had not yet been raised to a style and a moralism that had not yet broken past the rationalistic and conventional.)

The early stories hardly prepare one for the work to come. For with *The House of Mirth* (1905), a full-scale portrait of a lovely young woman trapped between her crass ambitions and her disabling refinements of sensibility, Mrs. Wharton composed one of the few American novels that approaches the finality of the tragic. The book is close in philosophic temper to European naturalism, though constructed with an eye toward "well-made" effects that are quite distant from the passion for accumulating evidence that we associate with the naturalistic novel. At its best Mrs. Wharton's style is terse, caustic, and epigrammatic—a prose of aggressive commentary and severe control. At points of emotional stress, however, she succumbs to a fault that is to mar all her novels except *The Age of Innocence:* she employs an overcharged rhetoric to impose upon her story complexities of meaning it cannot support and intensities of feeling it does not need. If not her most finished work, *The House of Mirth* is Mrs. Wharton's most powerful one, the novel in which she dramatizes, with a fullness and freedom she would never again command, her sense of the pervasiveness of waste in human affairs and the tyranny that circumstance can exert over human will and desire.

Technically, Mrs. Wharton was not an audacious writer. She felt little sympathy with the experiments that were being undertaken during her lifetime by the great European and American novelists. In reading her books one is always aware that for Mrs. Wharton the novel is essentially a fixed form, a closely designed if somewhat heavy container of narrative, the presence of which we are never invited to forget. For unlike such impressionist writers as Conrad and Faulkner, she does not seek for that illusion of transparency which might tempt a reader to suppose he is "in" the world of the novel. She wishes her audience always to be aware of her firm guiding hand, to regard it as a force of assurance and control. In the several senses of the term, she is a *formal* writer.

Mrs. Wharton composed the kind of novel in which the plot stands out in its own right, like a clear and visible line of intention; in which the characters are taken to be rationally apprehensible, coherent figures to be portrayed through their actions rather than dissolved into a stream of psychology; and in which the narrative point of view is quickly established and limited, even if most of the time it comes through the austere tones of Mrs. Wharton's own voice. Her locale and subject-matter are usually American, but her view of the possibilities and limitations of the novel as a form makes her seem closer to such Europeans as Flaubert than to Americans like Melville and Twain.

(She is a writer of limited scope. The historic span of her novels is narrow, usually confined to those late nineteenth century realignments of power and status that comprise a high moment in the biography of the American bourgeoisie. The social range is also narrow, dealing usually with clashes among segments of the rich or with personal relationships as these have been defined, or

distorted, by the conventions of a fixed society. Mrs. Wharton had
no gift for the large and "open" narrative forms, those sprawling
prose epics which in modern fiction have been employed to depict
large areas of national experience. Nor, despite an intense awareness
of the pressure of impulse in human life, does she care to encounter the murk and puzzle of the unconscious. She respects it,
she fears it, she would as soon keep it at a distance. The arena of
her imagination is the forefront of social life, where manners re-
veal moral stress or bias, and accepted forms of conduct may break
under the weight of personal desire. "Civilization and its discon-
tents"—the phrase from Freud could stand as an epigraph for her
books. She writes as a convinced rationalist, but in her best work
as a rationalist who knows how desperately besieged and vulnerable
human reason is.

Within these traditional limits, and despite her coolness to mod-
ernist innovations, Mrs. Wharton was a restless writer, forever
seeking new variations of tone and theme, and in her several important novels after *The House of Mirth* rarely troubling to repeat
a success. In *The Reef* (1912) she composed a subtle though tenuous
drama of personal relations, Jamesian in manner and diction,
which deals largely with the price and advantage of moral scruple.
In *The Custom of the Country* (1913) she turned to—I think it fair
to say, she was largely the innovator of—a tough-spirited, fierce, and
abrasive satire of the barbaric philistinism she felt to be settling
upon American society and the source of which she was inclined
to locate, not with complete accuracy, in the new raw towns of the
Midwest. Endless numbers of American novels would later be
written on this theme, and Sinclair Lewis would commonly be
mentioned as a writer particularly indebted to *The Custom of the
Country;* but the truth is that no American novelist of our time—
with the single exception of Nathanael West—has been so ruthless,
so bitingly cold as Mrs. Wharton in assaulting the vulgarities and
failures of our society. Her considerable gifts for caricature—what
Edmund Wilson calls her "method of doing crude and harsh people
with a draftsmanship crude and hard"—reached their fruition in
The Custom of the Country, a novel that is hard to endure because
it provides no consoling reconciliations and has therefore never been

properly valued or even widely read. (And finally in the list of her superior novels there is *The Age of Innocence* (1920), a suavely ironic evocation of New York in the 1870's, blending Mrs. Wharton's nostalgia for the world from which she came with her criticism of its genteel timidities and evasions. Simply as a piece of writing *The Age of Innocence* is Mrs. Wharton's masterpiece, for it is difficult to think of many American novels written in a prose so polished and supple.)

On occasion Mrs. Wharton was also a master of the shorter forms of prose fiction. A fine selection could be made from her short stories, and there are three short novels or novelettes—*Ethan Frome* (1911), *Summer* (1917) and *The Bunner Sisters* (1916)—which are of permanent interest. *Ethan Frome,* a severe depiction of gratuitous human suffering in a New England village, is a work meant to shock and depress; it has often been criticized, wrongly, for being so successfully the *tour de force* Mrs. Wharton meant it to be—that is, for leaving us with a sense of admiration for the visible rigor of its mechanics and a sense of pain because of its total assault upon our emotions. *Summer,* a more complex and thoughtful piece of writing, is also set in rural New England, displaying a close knowledge of locale and character which would surprise those who suppose Mrs. Wharton merely to be the chronicler of the New York rich. And *The Bunner Sisters,* an account of the sufferings of two poor women in New York, is not only a masterpiece of compressed realism but a notable example of Mrs. Wharton's ability to release through her fiction a disciplined compassion that is far more impressive than the rhetoric of protest cultivated by many liberal and radical writers. One or two other novelettes by Mrs. Wharton, such as the melodramatic *The Old Maid,* also have a certain interest, for the short novel was a form in which her fondness for economy of effects—a sweeping narrative line, a brisk prose, a rapid disposition of theme and figures—served her well.

The remaining novels? A few are dull and earnest failures, like *The Fruit of the Tree,* and too many others, like *The Glimpses of the Moon,* are barely superior to ladies' magazine fiction. In the novels written during the last fifteen years of her life, Mrs. Wharton's intellectual conservatism hardened into an embittered and querulous disdain for modern life; she no longer really knew what was happening in America; and she lost what had once been her main gift: the accurate location of the target she wished to destroy.

The Heiress of Henry James? One reason justice has not yet come to Edith Wharton is the widespread assumption that she is primarily a disciple of Henry James—a gifted disciple, to be sure, but not nearly so gifted as the master. Now it is true that if you come to Mrs. Wharton's work with the expectation of finding replicas of the Jamesian novel, you will probably be disappointed; but then the expectation itself is a mistake. (The claim that Henry James exerted a major influence upon Mrs. Wharton's fiction, repeated with maddening regularity by literary historians, testifies to the laziness of the human mind and in particular to the reluctance of scholars to suppose that anything can spring directly from the art of a writer without also having some clearly specifiable source in an earlier writer.)

The literary relationship between James and Mrs. Wharton is too complex to be fully examined here, but I should like to make a few assertions and dispute with a few of the critics who appear in this book. I contend that Mrs. Wharton is not primarily the disciple of James; that James's influence upon her work has either been overstated or misunderstood; and that, within certain obvious limits, she is an original writer.

In one large and pleasant way Mrs. Wharton did regard herself as permanently indebted to Henry James. For her, as for so many later writers, he loomed as a model of artistic conscience and selflessness; his example made their calling seem a sacred one, his devotion to craft made everything else seem trivial. James persuaded her that the composition of a novel should not be a mere outpouring, but a craft to be studied and mastered; he was, as she said in tribute, "about the only novelist who had formulated his ideas about his art." In this respect, then, James was her "inspiration"—which is something rather different from an influence.

There is *some* evidence of a direct literary influence. A number of James's early novels left their mark upon that side of Mrs. Wharton's work which is concerned with the comedy of social manners. To say this, however, is to indicate a serious qualification: for if James began as a novelist of manners he soon became something else as well, and although Mrs. Wharton was skillful at observing manners and in most of her books more dependent than James upon the use of such observation, it is finally for the strength of her personal vision and the incisiveness of her mind that we should value her work. Perhaps one could say that it was the lesser James that influenced the lesser Mrs. Wharton.

The point seems to be enforced by E. K. Brown when he writes that "The picture of the Faubourg Saint Germain in *Madame de Treymes* [a story by Mrs. Wharton] owes as much to [James's] *The American* and *Madame de Mauves* as it does to direct observation." This is largely correct, but it affects only some minor instances of Mrs. Wharton's work and is not sufficient ground for the usual claim of a pervasive Jamesian influence. Brown is also correct in noting that "from the beginning to the end *The Reef* is Jamesian." Yet here too qualifications are needed: the refined agonies of conscience which Anna Leath experiences in this novel are of a kind that depend on Mrs. Wharton's "feminine" side and thereby are mostly beyond the reach of James, while the ending of the novel, so painfully tendentious and damaging to all that has preceded it, is also dependent on Mrs. Wharton's "feminine" side, as this time it takes upon itself the privilege of moral retaliation. Still, the fact of differences between two writers does not remove the possibility of influence, and in regard to *The Reef* that influence is clear.

Can we go any further? In her valuable essay Q. D. Leavis cites Mrs. Wharton's remark that James "belonged irrevocably to the old America out of which I also came," and that he was "essentially a novelist of manners, and the manners he was qualified by nature and situation to observe were those of the little vanishing group of people among whom he had grown up." Such statements form part of Mrs. Leavis's ground for calling Edith Wharton "the heiress of Henry James," but in taking those statements at face value she is, I think, being led somewhat astray.

Mrs. Wharton's description of James's novels is clearly inadequate, for it transforms him into a writer excessively like herself. His dependence on the manners of "the little vanishing group of people among whom he had grown up" was never very great and, as his art matured, was left almost entirely behind. And though a figure of "the old America," James came from a milieu quite different from the one in which Mrs. Wharton was raised and upon which she drew so heavily in her fiction. Though a New Yorker by birth and occasional residence, James had his closest ties of intellect and temperament with the New England of philosophical idealism, both as it came down to him in its own right and as it was recast in the speculations of his father Henry James, Sr. Now it is precisely this element of American thought to which the mind of Mrs. Wharton was closed: both to her literary profit, since she escaped its vapidity, and her literary loss, since a major lack in her writing is any trace of that urge to transcendence, that glow of the vision of the possible, which lights up even the darkest of James's novels.

The intellectual backgrounds of the two writers are quite different, and that is one reason Mrs. Wharton could not respond favorably to James's later novels. The whole Emersonian tradition, so important a formative element in James's sensibility and so pervasive in his later books, was alien to her. E. K. Brown has noted this difference in more personal terms:

> Edith Wharton both in her life and her work seemed to have missed happiness. Something tense and thin and a little sharp marked both. . . . Beneath all the tensions of James, there was a place where life was sweet and warm; and despite the nervous precisions of his style . . . there was something large and rich about his work which is absent from that of [Mrs. Wharton].

The truth is that in Mrs. Wharton's most important novels it is hard to detect any *specific* Jamesian influence. Perhaps it can be found in her conception of the novel as a form, her wish to write with plan and economy; perhaps in the style of *The Custom of the Country,* which may owe something to the cold brilliance of James's prose in *The Bostonians.* But Mrs. Wharton's novelettes are in setting, theme, and characterization quite alien to James, while each of her three best novels—*The House of Mirth, The Custom of the Country* and *The Age of Innocence*—is a work notably different from either the early or late James. The somewhat naturalistic method of *The House of Mirth* and Mrs. Wharton's preoccupation with Lily Bart as victim of her social milieu, the caustic satire of *The Custom of the Country* and Mrs. Wharton's impatience with its feeble hero as an agent of traditional values, the modulated style of *The Age of Innocence* and Mrs. Wharton's complex involvement with the world of her birth—all this seems her own. Her characteristic style is sharper, clearer, more aggressive, and less metaphorical than James's in all but a few of his novels. Her narrative line is usually more direct than his. And her sense of life is more despondent, less open to the idea or even the possibility of redemption.

A World and Its Changes. Mrs. Wharton's best novels portray the life of New York during the latter third of the nineteenth century. Economically and socially, this world was dominated by an established wealthy class consisting of the sons and grandsons of energetic provincial merchants. In the 1870's and 1880's this class did not yet feel seriously threatened by the competition and clamor of the *nouveaux riches;* it had gained enough wealth to care about leisure, and enough leisure to think of setting itself up as a modest aristocracy. The phrase *modest aristocracy* may seem a contradiction in terms, but it should serve to suggest the difficulty of building an enclave of social precedence in the fluid bourgeois society America was then becoming or had, indeed, already become.

Quite free from any disturbing intensities of belief or aspirations toward grandeur of style, this class was strict in its decorum and narrow in its conventions. With tepid steadfastness it devoted itself to good manners, good English, good form. And it cared about culture too—culture as a static and finished quantity, something one had to possess but did not have to live by. Its one great passion was to be left alone, unchallenged and untroubled by the motions of history; and this of course was the one privilege history could not bestow. The nation was becoming industrialized; waves of immigrants were descending upon New York; financial empires were being established in the alien cities of the Midwest as well as in Wall Street itself. Such developments made it inevitable that the provincial ruling class of "old New York" should suffer both assault and assimilation by newer, more vigorous, and less cultivated segments of the American bourgeoisie.

In his charming memoir, *Portrait of Edith Wharton,* Percy Lubbock has left a description of "old New York" which blends irony and affection in a manner somewhat like Mrs. Wharton's own:

Her New York . . . has there the appearance of a well-rounded polity, as compact within its circuit as an old walled township, *la cité antique,* before the days of spreading suburbs and liberties without the gates: such was the comfortable self-containment of its life. . . . [It was] a society conscious of itself, aware of its order, sufficient for its needs, beyond any to be seen today, or perhaps in its own day either. It was in no way large enough to be unwieldy or out of hand. It had its choice traditions, not old enough to have loosened or diverged; its organized forms, too plain to be ignored; its customary law, too distinct and categorical to be evaded. I have heard that Edith's mother, a high authority on the subject, would count the names of all the families, in due order of degree, who composed the world to which her daughter was born; and there her world stopped short, it was implied, and no mistake about it.

In "old New York" no one soared and no one was supposed, visibly, to sink. Leisure ruled. Husbands rarely went to their offices "downtown," and there were long midday lunches and solemn entertainments in the evening. Good conversation, though of a not too taxing kind, was felt to be desirable. Taste and form were the reigning gods, not the less tyrannical for their apparent mildness of administration. As Mrs. Wharton remarked with gentle sarcasm in *The Age of Innocence,* it was a world composed of people "who dreaded scandal more than disease, who placed decency above courage, and who considered that nothing was more ill-bred than 'scenes,' except the behavior of those who gave rise to them." In the same novel she wrote: "What was or was not 'the thing' played a part as important in Newland Archer's New York as the inscrutable totem terrors that had ruled the destinies of his forefathers thousands of years ago." And above all, "old New York" was a world that had entered its decline. What was happening in the years of Mrs. Wharton's youth, as Louis Auchincloss remarks, was "the assault upon an old and conservative group by the multitudes enriched, and fabulously enriched, by the business expansion of the preceding decades." Mrs. Wharton kept returning to this theme, half in the cool spirit of the anthropologist studying the death of a tribe, half with the nostalgia of a survivor mourning the loss of vanished graces.

Toward the world in which she grew up Mrs. Wharton retained a mixture of feelings that anticipates those of later American writers toward their immigrant childhood and youth in a new New York. It was too fatally *her* world, beyond choice or escape, and it would serve her as lifelong memory, lifelong subject, perhaps lifelong trauma. She loved "old New York" with that mixture of grieving affection and protective impatience Faulkner would later feel toward Mississippi and Saul Bellow toward the Jewish neighborhoods of Chicago. Yet it also left her dissatisfied, on edge, unfulfilled. Her work, as Edmund Wilson has remarked, "was . . . the desperate product of a pressure of [personal] maladjustments. . . . At her strongest and most characteristic, she is a brilliant example of the writer who relieves an emotional strain by denouncing his generation." For she yearned for a way of life that might bring greater intellectual risks and yield greater emotional rewards than her family and friends could imagine, and only after a time did she find it in her dedication to writing. Just as Faulkner's attitudes toward his home country have kept shifting from one ambiguity to another, so Mrs. Wharton combined toward her home city feelings both of harsh rejection and haughty defense. There are moments, especially in *The House of Mirth,* when she is utterly without mercy toward "old New York": she sees it as a place of betrayal, failure, and impotence. In her old age, when she came to write her autobiography, she was mellower—though perhaps the word should really be, harder—in spirit. "It used to seem to me," she wrote, "that the group in which I grew up was like an empty vessel into which no new wine would ever again be poured. Now I see that one of its uses lay in preserving a few drops of an old vintage too rare to be savored by a youthful palate. . . ."

For a novelist to be so profoundly involved with a known and measured society offers many advantages. Mrs. Wharton wrote about her segment of America with an authority few novelists could surpass, for she was one of the two or three among them who knew, fully and from the inside, what the life of the rich in this country was really like. Henry James had used that life as an occasion for fables of freedom and circumstance in his later books; F. Scott Fitzgerald, an interloper in the world of wealth, was to collect brilliant guesses and fragments of envious insight; John O'Hara has felt his way along the provincial outposts of the America that made its money late and fast. But no American writer has known quite so deeply as Mrs. Wharton what it means, both as privilege and burden, to grow up in a family of the established rich: a family where there was enough money and had been money long enough for talk about it to seem vulgar, and where conspicuous effort to make more of it seemed still more vulgar. While a final critical estimate of her novels can hardly rest on such considerations alone, one reason for continuing to read *The House of Mirth, The Custom of the Country,* and *The Age of Innocence* is the shrewdness with which Mrs. Wharton, through an expert scrutiny of manners, is able to discriminate among the gradations of power and status in the world of the rich. To read these books is to discover how the novel of manners can register both the surface of social life and the inner vibrations of spirit that surface reveals, suppresses, and distorts.

There were other advantages in being so close to her materials. As with Faulkner, the subject seems to have chosen the writer, not the writer the subject; everything came to her with the pressure and inexorability of a felt memory; each return to the locale of her youth raised the possibility of a new essay at self-discovery. And in books like *The House of Mirth* and *The Age of Innocence* she could work on the assumption, so valuable to a writer who prizes economy of structure, that moral values can be tested in a novel by dramatizing the relationships between fixed social groups and mobile characters. In the friction thus engendered, moral values come to be seen not as abstract categories imposed upon human experience but as problems, elements in the effort of men to cope with conflicting desires and obligations. At every point in *The House of Mirth* the history of Lily Bart is defined by her journey from one social group to another, a journey both she and her friends regard as a fall but which she, after great confusion and pain, comes to see may have positive consequences. Because Mrs. Wharton is so completely in control of her material, the meanings of the book emerge through a series of contrasts between a fixed scale of social place and an evolving measure of moral value.

But as she herself knew quite well, there was little in Mrs. Wharton's world that could provide her with a subject large in social scope and visibly tragic in its implications. Had "old New York" gone down in blind and bitter resistance to the *nouveauv riches,* that might have been a subject appropriate to moral or social tragedy; but since there was far less conflict than fusion between the old money and the new, she had little alternative to the varieties of comedy that dominate her books. Only once in her novels did she achieve a tragic resonance, and that was in *The House of Mirth* where Lily Bart is shown as the victim of a world that had made possible her loveliness and inevitable her limitations. Even here we must reduce the traditional notion of the tragic to the pathetic on one side and bleak on the other, if the term is to be used with approximate relevance. In discussing this novel Mrs. Wharton showed a complete awareness of her problem. How, she asked herself, "could a society of irresponsible pleasure-seekers be said to have, on the 'old woes of the world,' any deeper bearing than the people composing such a society could guess?" And she answered: "A frivolous society can acquire dramatic significance only through what its frivolity destroys. Its tragic implication lies in its power of debasing people and ideas."

Toward the end of her career Mrs. Wharton found it more and more difficult to employ her material with the success that marks her work between 1905 and 1920. Her later novels are shoddy and sometimes mean-spirited in the hauteur with which she dismisses younger generations beyond the reach of her understanding or sympathy. These novels bristle with her impatience before the mysteries of a world she could not enter, the world of twentieth century America, and are notable for a truculence of temper, a hardening of the moral arteries. I would offer the speculation that Mrs. Wharton, whose intelligence should never be underestimated, was aware that the ground on which she took her moral stand was dissolving beneath her. At best the world of her youth had been an aristocracy of surface ("In that simple society," she recalled, "there was an almost pagan worship of physical beauty"), but she had always wanted it to be something better—something beautiful and truly distinguished. She had wanted to look upon it as potentially an aristocracy of value, and throughout most of her life she struggled with this desire and her recognition that it was an impossible, even unreasonable desire. But even when she recognized this, she still wondered to what extent the style and decorum of "old New York" had at least made possible some of the aspirations she had cherished since childhood. Having a thoroughly earthbound mind, she sought for tangible embodiments, in social groups or communities, of the values to which she clung—for she could not be content with the fabulous imaginings Henry James spun in his later novels. She turned, at times with open savagery and at other times with a feeling as close to wistfulness as she could tolerate, to the world of her birth, hoping to find there some token of security by which to satisfy the needs of her imagination. In the inevitable disappointment that followed, Mrs. Wharton, though extremely conservative in her opinions, proved to be the American novelist least merciful in her treatment of the rich. She kept harassing them, nagging at them in a language they could not, with the best will in the world, understand; and then she became glacial in her contempt, almost too willing to slash away at their mediocrity because she did not know anyone else to turn toward or against.

At the end she was alone. If the incongruity between desire and realization is a recurrent motif in her writing about personal relationships, it is an incongruity she also observed in her dealings with the public world. There were always available to her, once she settled in France, a number of personal friends, men and women of high if somewhat forbidding culture. But what emerges from a scrutiny of her work as a whole is that Mrs. Wharton, like so many of those younger deracinated novelists who both interested and disturbed her, was a solitary, clinging to values for which she could find no place, and holding fast, with tight-lipped stoicism, to the nerve of her pride. She was a writer haunted by what she disliked, haunted by the demons of modernism as they encircled her both in life and literature. She would have nothing to do with them, yet in her most important books they kept reappearing, both as agents of moral dissolution and as possibilities of fresh life that needed to be kept sternly in check.

A Personal Vision. The texture of Mrs. Wharton's novels is dark. Like so many writers whose education occurred during the latter decades of the nineteenth century, she felt that the universe—which for her is virtually to say, organized society—was profoundly inhospitable to human need and desire. The malaise which troubled so many intelligent people during her lifetime—the feeling that they were living in an age when energies had run down, meanings collapsed, and the flow of organic life been replaced by the sterile and mechanical—is quite as acute in her novels as in those of Hardy and Gissing. Like them, she felt that somehow the world had hardened and turned cold, and she could find no vantage point at which to establish a protective distance from it. This condition is somewhat different from the strain of melancholy that runs through American literature, surely different from the metaphysical despera-tion that overcame Melville in his later years or the misanthropy that beset Twain. What Mrs. Wharton felt was more distinctly "European" in quality, more related to that rationalist conservatism which is a perennial motif in French intellectual life and manifests itself as a confirmed skepticism about the possibilties of human relationships.

In many of Mrs. Wharton's novels there recur what Blake Nevius has called

> two complex and basically unresolvable themes. The first is provided
> by the spectacle of a large and generous nature . . . trapped by cir-
> cumstances ironically of its own devising into consanguinity with a
> meaner nature. . . . There is no accounting for such disastrous unions
> except as a result of the generous but misguided impulses of the larger
> nature; there is no justifying their waste of human resources. More-
> over, there is no evading the responsibility they entail, and this
> acknowledgment . . . opens the way for her second theme. . . . [She]
> tries to define the nature and limits of individual responsibility, to
> determine what allowance of freedom or rebellion can be made for
> her trapped protagonist without at the same time threatening the
> structure of society.

In Mrs. Wharton's vision of things—and we can only speculate on the extent to which her personal unhappiness contributed to it —human beings seem always to prove inadequate, always to fail each other, always to be the victims of an innate disharmony be-tween love and response, need and capacity. Men especially have a hard time of it in Mrs. Wharton's novels. In their notorious vanity and faithlessness, they seldom "come through"; they fail Mrs. Wharton's heroines less from bad faith than from weak imagination, a laziness of spirit that keeps them from a true grasp of suffering; and in a number of her novels one finds a suppressed feminine bitterness, a profound impatience with the claims of the ruling sex. This feminist resentment seems, in turn, only an instance of what Mrs. Wharton felt to be a more radical and galling inequity at the heart of the human scheme. The inability of human beings to achieve self-sufficiency drives them to seek relationships with other people, and these relationships necessarily compromise their freedom by subjecting them to the pain of a desire either too great or too small. Things, in Mrs. Wharton's world, do not work out. In one of her books she speaks of "the sense of mortality," and of "its loneliness, the way it must be borne without help." I am convinced she meant by this more than the prospect of death. What "must be borne without help" is the inexorable disarrangement of everything we seek through intelligence and will to arrange.

Mrs. Wharton's general hostility toward "modern" ideas must have predisposed her against Freudian psychology, yet one is repeatedly struck by the fact that, at least in regard to the *possibilities* of the human enterprise, there is an underlying closeness of skepticism between her assumptions and Freud's theories. Mrs. Wharton had a highly developed, perhaps overdeveloped, sense of the power of everything in organized social existence which checks our desires. Like Freud, she believed that we must endure an irremediable conflict between nature and culture, and although she had at least as healthy a respect as he did for the uses of sublimation, she also knew that the human capacity for putting up with substitute gratifications is limited. From this impasse—what Philip Rieff, in discussing Freud, has called "the painful snare of contradiction in which nature and culture, individual and society, are forever fixed" —she could see no easy way out.

A good many of Mrs. Wharton's critics have assumed that she was simply a defender of harsh social conventions against all those who, from romantic energy or mere hunger for meaning in life, rebel against the fixed patterns of their world. But this is not quite true for many of her books, and in regard to some of them not true at all. What is true is that most of her plots focus upon a clash between a stable society and a sensitive person who half belongs to and half rebels against it. At the end he must surrender to the social taboos he had momentarily challenged or wished to challenge, for he either has not been able to summon the resources of courage through which to act out his rebellion, or he has discovered that the punitive power of society is greater than he had supposed, or he has learned that the conventions he had assumed to be lifeless still retain a certain wisdom. Yet much of Mrs. Wharton's work contains a somewhat chill and detached sympathy for those very rebels in whose crushing she seems to connive. Her sense of the world is hardly such as to persuade her of its goodness; it is merely such as to persuade her of its force.

Mrs. Wharton understands how large is the price, how endless the nagging pain, that must be paid for a personal assertion against the familiar ways of the world, and she believes, simply, that most of us lack the strength to pay. Yet she has no respect for blind acceptance, and time after time expresses her distaste for "sterile pain" and "the vanity of self-sacrifice." It is hard to imagine another writer in American literature for whom society, despite its attractions of surface and order, figures so thoroughly as a prison of the human soul. And there, she seems to say, there it is: the doors locked, the bars firm. "Life," she wrote in *The Fruit of the Tree,* "is not a matter of abstract principles, but a succession of pitiful compromises with fate, of concessions to old traditions, old beliefs, old tragedies, old failures."

This sense of fatality has, in her best work, a certain minor magnificence, what might be called the magnificence of the bleak. As Edmund Wilson remarks:

> she combines with indignation against a specific phase of American society a general sense of inexorable doom for human beings. She was much haunted by the myth of the Eumenides; and she has developed her own deadly version of the working of the Aeschylean necessity—a version as automatic and rapid, as decisive and as undimmed by sentiment, as the mechanical and financial processes which during her lifetime were transforming New York. . . .

In a final reckoning, of course, Mrs. Wharton's vision of life has its severe limitations. She knew only too well how experience can grind men into hopelessness, how it can leave them persuaded that the need for choice contains within itself the seeds of tragedy and the impossibility of choice the sources of pain. Everything that reveals the power of the conditioned, everything that shreds our aspirations, she brought to full novelistic life. Where she failed was in giving imaginative embodiment to the human will seeking to

resist defeat or move beyond it. She lacked James's ultimate serenity.
She lacked his gift for summoning in images of conduct the purity
of children and the selflessness of girls. She lacked the vocabulary
of happiness.

But whatever Mrs. Wharton could see, she looked at with absolute courage. She believed that what the heart desires brings with
it a price—and often an exorbitant price. Americans are not trained
to accept this view of the human situation, and there is nothing to
recommend it except the fact that it contains at least a fraction of
the truth. How well, with what sardonic pleasure, Mrs. Wharton
would have responded to the lines of W. H. Auden:

> Every farthing of the cost
> All the bitter stars foretell
> Shall be paid.

Justice to Edith Wharton

by Edmund Wilson

Before Edith Wharton died, the more commonplace work of her later years had had the effect of dulling the reputation of her earlier and more serious work. It seemed to me that the notices elicited by her death did her, in general, something less than justice; and I want to try to throw into relief the achievements which did make her important during a period—say, 1905-1917—when there were few American writers worth reading. This essay is therefore no very complete study, but rather in the nature of an impression by a reader who was growing up at that time.

Mrs. Wharton's earliest fiction I never found particularly attractive. The influences of Paul Bourget and Henry James seem to have presided at the birth of her talent; and I remember these books as dealing with the artificial moral problems of Bourget and developing them with the tenuity of analysis which is what is least satisfactory in James. The stories tended to take place either in a social void or against a background of Italy or France which had somewhat the character of expensive upholstery. It was only with *The House of Mirth*, published in 1905, that Edith Wharton emerged as an historian of the American society of her time. For a period of fifteen years or more, she produced work of considerable interest both for its realism and its intensity.

One has heard various accounts of her literary beginnings. She tells us in her autobiography that a novel which she had composed at eleven and which began, "Oh, how do you do, Mrs. Brown? . . .

If only I had known you were going to call, I should have tidied up the drawing room"—had been returned by her mother with the chilling comment, "Drawing rooms are always tidy." And it is said that a book of verse which she had written and had had secretly printed was discovered and destroyed by her parents, well-to-do New Yorkers of merchant stock, who thought it unladylike for a young woman to write. It seems to be an authentic fact—though Mrs. Wharton does not mention it in her memoirs—that she first seriously began to write fiction after her marriage, during the period of a nervous breakdown, at the suggestion of Dr. S. Weir Mitchell, who himself combined the practice of literature with his pioneer work in the field of female neuroses. Thereafter she seems to have depended on her writing to get her through some difficult years, a situation that became more and more painful. Her husband, as she tells us, had some mental disease which was steadily growing worse from the very first years of their marriage, and he inhabited a social world of the rich which was sealed tight to intellectual interests. Through her writing, she came gradually into relation with the international literary world and made herself a partially independent career.

Her work was, then, the desperate product of a pressure of maladjustments; and it very soon took a direction totally different from that of Henry James, as a lesser disciple of whom she is sometimes pointlessly listed. James's interests were predominantly esthetic: he is never a passionate social prophet; and only rarely—as in *The Ivory Tower*, which seems in turn to have derived from Mrs. Wharton—does he satirize plutocratic America. But a passionate social prophet is precisely what Edith Wharton became. At her strongest and most characteristic, she is a brilliant example of the writer who relieves an emotional strain by denouncing his generation.

It is true that she combines with indignation against a specific phase of American society a general sense of inexorable doom for human beings. She was much haunted by the myth of the Eumenides; and she had developed her own deadly version of the working of the Aeschylean necessity—a version as automatic and rapid, as decisive and as undimmed by sentiment, as the mechanical and financial processes which during her lifetime were transforming New York. In these books, she was as pessimistic as Hardy or Maupassant.

You find the pure expression of her hopelessness in her volume of poems, *Artemis to Actaeon*, published in 1909, which, for all its hard accent and its ponderous tone, its "impenetrables" and "incommunicables" and "incommensurables," its "immemorial altitudes august," was not entirely without interest or merit. "Death, can it be the years shall naught avail?" she asks in one of the sonnets called *Experience*: " 'Not so,' Death answered. 'They shall purchase sleep.' " But in the poem called *Moonrise over Tyringham*, she seems to be emerging from a period of strain into a relatively tranquil stoicism. She is apostrophizing the first hour of night:

> Be thou the image of a thought that fares
> Forth from itself, and flings its ray ahead,
> Leaping the barriers of ephemeral cares,
> To where our lives are but the ages' tread,
>
> And let this year be, not the last of youth,
> But first—like thee!—of some new train of hours,
> If more remote from hope, yet nearer truth,
> And kin to the unpetitionable powers.

But the catastrophe in Edith Wharton's novels is almost invariably the upshot of a conflict between the individual and the social group. Her tragic heroines and heroes are the victims of the group pressure of convention; they are passionate or imaginative spirits, hungry for emotional and intellectual experience, who find themselves locked into a small closed system, and either destroy themselves by beating their heads against their prison or suffer a living death in resigning themselves to it. Out of these themes she got a sharp pathos all her own. The language and some of the machinery of *The House of Mirth* seem old-fashioned and rather melodramatic today; but the book had some originality and power, with its chronicle of a social parasite on the fringes of the very rich, dragging out a stupefying routine of week-ends, yachting trips and dinners, and finding a window open only twice, at the beginning and at the end of the book, on a world where all the values are not money values.

The Fruit of the Tree, which followed it in 1907, although its characters are concerned with larger issues, is less successful than

The House of Mirth, because it is confused between two different kinds of themes. There is a more or less trumped-up moral problem à la Bourget about a "mercy killing" by a high-minded trained nurse, who happened to have an "affinity," as they used to say at that period, with the husband of the patient. But there is also the story of an industrial reformer, which is on the whole quite ably handled—especially in the opening scenes, in which the hero, assistant manager of a textile mill, is aroused by an industrial accident to try to remove the conditions which have caused it and finds himself up against one of those tight family groups that often dominate American factory towns, sitting ensconced in their red-satin drawing rooms on massively upholstered sofas, amid heavy bronze chandeliers and mantels surmounted by obelisk clocks; and in its picture of his marriage with the mill-owning widow and the gradual drugging of his purpose under the influence of a house on Long Island of a quality more gracious and engaging but on an equally overpowering scale.

Edith Wharton had come to have a great hand with all kinds of American furnishings and with their concomitant landscape-gardening. Her first book had been a work on interior decorating; and now in her novels she adopts the practice of inventorying the contents of her characters' homes. Only Clyde Fitch, I think, in those early 1900's made play to the same degree with the miscellaneous material objects with which Americans were surrounding themselves—articles which had just been manufactured and which people were being induced to buy. I suppose that no other writer of comedies of any other place or time has depended so much on stage sets and, especially, on stage properties: the radiators that bang in *Girls,* the artificial orange in *The Truth,* the things that are dropped under the table by the ladies in the second act of *The Climbers.* But in the case of Edith Wharton, the decors become the agents of tragedy. The characters of Clyde Fitch are embarrassed or tripped up by these articles; but the people of Edith Wharton are pursued by them as by spirits of doom and ultimately crushed by their accumulation. These pieces have not been always made newly: sometimes they are *objets d'art,* which have been expensively imported from Europe. But the effect is very much the same: they are something extraneous to the people and, no matter how old they may be, they seem to glitter and clank with the coin that has gone to buy them. A great many of Mrs. Wharton's descriptions are, of course, satiric or caustic; but when she wants to produce an impression of real magnificence, and even when she is writing about Europe, the thing still seems rather inorganic. She was not only one of the great pioneers, but also the poet, of interior decoration.

In *The Custom of the Country* (1913), Mrs. Wharton's next novel about the rich—*The Reef* is a relapse into "psychological problems"—she piles up the new luxury of the era to an altitude of ironic grandeur, like the glass mountain in the *Arabian Nights*, which the current of her imagination manages to make incandescent. The first scene sets the key for the whole book:

> Mrs. Spragg and her visitor were enthroned in two heavy gilt arm-chairs in one of the private drawing-rooms of the Hotel Stentorian. The Spragg rooms were known as one of the Looey suites, and the drawing room walls, above their wainscoting of highly varnished mahogany, were hung with salmon-pink damask and adorned with oval portraits of Marie Antoinette and the Princess de Lamballe. In the center of the florid carpet a gilt table with a top of Mexican onyx sustained a palm in a gilt basket tied with a pink bow. But for this ornament, and a copy of *The Hound of the Baskervilles* which lay beside it, the room showed no traces of human use, and Mrs. Spragg herself wore as complete an air of detachment as if she had been a wax figure in a show-window.

In the last pages—it is an admirable passage—Undine Spragg's little boy is seen wandering alone amid the splendors of the Paris *hôtel* which has crowned his mother's progress from the Stentorian:

> the white fur rugs and brocade chairs . . . [which] . . . seemed maliciously on the watch for smears and ink-spots, . . . his mother's wonderful lacy bedroom, all pale silks and velvets, artful mirrors and veiled lamps, and the boudoir as big as a drawing room, with pictures he would have liked to know about, and tables and cabinets holding things he was afraid to touch, . . . [the library, with its] . . . rows and rows of books, bound in dim browns and golds, and old faded reds as rich as velvet: they all looked as if they might have had stories in them as splendid as their bindings. But the bookcases were closed with gilt trellising, and when Paul reached up to open one, a servant told him that Mr. Moffatt's secretary kept them locked because the books were too valuable to be taken down.

It is a vein which Sinclair Lewis has worked since—as in the opening pages of *Babbitt*, where Babbitt is shown entangled with his gadgets; and in other respects *The Custom of the Country* opens up the way for Lewis, who dedicated *Main Street* to Edith Wharton. Mrs. Wharton has already arrived at a method of doing crude and harsh people with a draftsmanship crude and harsh. Undine Spragg, the social-climbing divorcée, though a good deal less humanly credible than Lily Bart of *The House of Mirth*, is quite a successful caricature of a type who was to go even farther. She is the prototype in fiction of the "gold-digger," of the international cocktail bitch. Here the pathos has been largely subordinated to an implacable animosity toward the heroine; but there is one episode both bitter and poignant, in which a discarded husband of Undine's, who has been driven by her demands to work in Wall Street and left by her up to his neck in debt, goes home to Washington Square through "the heat, the noise, the smells of disheveled midsummer" New York, climbs to the room at the top of the house where he has kept his books and other things from college, and shoots himself there.

The other side of this world of wealth, which annihilates every impulse toward excellence, is a poverty which also annihilates. The writer of one of the notices on Mrs. Wharton's death was mistaken in assuming that *Ethan Frome* was a single uncharacteristic excursion outside the top social strata. It is true that she knew the top strata better than she knew anything else; but both in *The House of Mirth* and *The Fruit of the Tree* she is always aware of the pit of misery which is implied by the wastefulness of the plutocracy, and the horror or the fear of this pit is one of the forces that determine the action. There is a Puritan in Edith Wharton, and this Puritan is always insisting that we must face the unpleasant and the ugly. Not to do so is one of the worst sins in her morality; sybarites like Mr. Langhope in *The Fruit of the Tree*, amusing himself with a dilettante archaeology on his income from a badly-managed factory, like the fatuous mother of *Twilight Sleep*, who feels so safe with her facial massage and her Yogi, while her family goes to pieces under her nose, are among the characters whom she treats with most scorn. And the three novels I have touched on above were paralleled by another series—*Ethan Frome, The Bunner Sisters* and *Summer*—which dealt with milieux of a different kind.

Ethan Frome is still much read and well-known; but *The Bunner Sisters* has been undeservedly neglected. It is the last piece in the volume called *Xingu* (1916), a short novel about the length of *Ethan Frome*. This story of two small shopkeepers on Stuyvesant Square and a drug-addict clockmaker from Hoboken, involved in a relationship like a triple noose which will gradually choke them all, is one of the most terrible things that Edith Wharton ever wrote; and the last page, in which the surviving sister, her lifelong companion gone and her poor little business lost, sets out to look for a job, seems to mark the grimmest moment of Edith Wharton's darkest years. Here is not even the grandeur of the heroic New England hills:

> "'Ain't you going to leave the *ad*-dress?' the young woman called out after her. Ann Eliza went out into the thronged street. The great city, under the fair spring sky, seemed to throb with the stir of innumerable beginnings. She walked on, looking for another shop window with a sign in it."

Summer (1917), however, returns to the Massachusetts of *Ethan Frome*, and, though neither so harrowing nor so vivid, is by no means an inferior work. Making hats in a millinery shop was the abyss from which Lily Bart recoiled; the heroine of *Summer* recoils from the nethermost American social stratum, the degenerate "mountain people." Let down by the refined young man who works in the public library and wants to become an architect, in a way that anticipates the situation in Dreiser's *An American Tragedy*, she finds that she cannot go back to her own people and allows herself to be made an honest woman by the rather admirable old failure of a lawyer who had brought her down from the mountain in her childhood. It is the first sign on Mrs. Wharton's part of a relenting in the cruelty of her endings. "Come to my age," says Charity Royall's protector, "a man knows the things that matter and the things that don't; that's about the only good turn life does us." Her blinding bitterness is already subsiding.

But in the meantime, before *Summer* was written, she had escaped from the hopeless situation created by her husband's insanity.

The doctors had told her he was hopeless; but she had had difficulty in inducing his family to allow her to leave him with an attendant. The tragedy of *The Bunner Sisters* is probably a transposition of this; and the relief of the tension in *Summer* is evidently the result of her new freedom. She was at last finally detached from her marriage; and she took up her permanent residence in France. The war came, and she threw herself into its activities.

And now the intensity dies from her work as the American background fades. One can see this already in *Summer,* and *The Age of Innocence* (1920) is really Edith Wharton's valedictory. The theme is closely related to those of *The House of Mirth* and *Ethan Frome*: the frustration of a potential pair of lovers by social or domestic obstructions. But setting it back in the generation of her parents, she is able to contemplate it now without quite the same rancor, to soften it with a poetic mist of distance. And yet even here the old impulse of protest still makes itself felt as the main motive. If we compare *The Age of Innocence* with Henry James's *Europeans,* whose central situation it reproduces, the pupil's divergence from the master is seen in the most striking way. In both cases, a Europeanized American woman—Baroness Münster, Countess Olenska—returns to the United States to intrude upon and disturb the existence of a conservative provincial society; in both cases, she attracts and almost captivates an intelligent man of the community who turns out, in the long run, to be unable to muster the courage to take her, and who allows her to go back to Europe. Henry James makes of this a balanced comedy of the conflict between the Bostonian and the cosmopolitan points of view (so he reproached her with not having developed the theme of Undine Spragg's marriage with a French nobleman in terms of French and American manners, as he had done with a similar one in *The Reverberator*); but in Edith Wharton's version one still feels an active resentment against the pusillanimity of the provincial group and also, as in other of her books, a special complaint against the timid American male who has let the lady down.

Up through *The Age of Innocence,* and recurring at all points of her range from *The House of Mirth* to *Ethan Frome,* the typical masculine figure in Edith Wharton's fiction is a man set apart from his neighbors by education, intellect, and feeling, but lacking the force or the courage either to impose himself or to get away. She generalizes about this type in the form in which she knew it best in her autobiographical volume: "They combined a cultivated taste with marked social gifts," she says; but "their weakness was that, save in a few cases, they made so little use of their ability": they were content to "live in dilettantish leisure," rendering none of "the public services that a more enlightened social system would have exacted of them." But she had described a very common phenomenon of the America of after the Civil War. Lawrence Selden, the city lawyer, who sits comfortably in his bachelor apartment with his flowerbox of mignonette and his first edition of La Bruyère and allows Lily Bart to drown, is the same person as Lawyer Royall of *Summer,* with his lofty orations and his drunken lapses. One could have found him during the big-business era in almost any American city or town: the man of superior abilities who had the impulse toward self-improvement and independence, but who had been more or less rendered helpless by the surf of headlong money-making and spending which carried him along with its breakers or left him stranded on the New England hills—in either case thwarted and stunted by the mediocre level of the community. In Edith Wharton's novels these men are usually captured and dominated by women of conventional morals and middle-class ideals; when an exceptional woman comes along who is thirsting for something different and better, the man is unable to give it to her. This special situation Mrs. Wharton, with some conscious historical criticism but chiefly impelled by a feminine animus, has dramatized with much vividness and intelligence. There are no first-rate men in these novels.

The Age of Innocence is already rather faded. But now a surprising lapse occurs. (It is true that she is nearly sixty.)

When we look back on Mrs. Wharton's career, it seems that everything that is valuable in her work lies within a quite sharply delimited area—between *The House of Mirth* and *The Age of Innocence.* It is sometimes true of women writers—less often, I believe, of men—that a manifestation of something like genius may be stimulated by some exceptional emotional strain, but will disappear when the stimulus has passed. With a man, his professional, his

artisan's life is likely to persist and evolve as a partially independent
organism through the vicissitudes of his emotional experience.
Henry James in a virtual vacuum continued to possess and develop
his *métier* up to his very last years. But Mrs. Wharton had no *métier*
in this sense. With her emergence from her life in the United States,
her settling down in the congenial society of Paris, she seems at
last to become comfortably adjusted; and with her adjustment, the
real intellectual force which she has exerted through a decade and
a half evaporates almost completely. She no longer maims or
massacres her characters. Her grimness melts rapidly into benignity.
She takes an interest in young people's problems, in the solicitude
of parents for children; she smooths over the misunderstandings of
lovers; she sees how things may work out very well. She even loses
the style she has mastered. Beginning with a language rather ponderous and stiff, the worst features of the style of Henry James and
a stream of clichés from old novels and plays, she finally—about the
time of *Ethan Frome*—worked out a prose of flexible steel, bright
as electric light and striking out sparks of wit and color, which has
the quality and pace of New York and is one of its distinctive
artistic products. But now not merely does she cease to be brilliant,
she becomes almost commonplace.

The Glimpses of the Moon, which followed *The Age of Innocence,*
is, as someone has said, scarcely distinguishable from the ordinary
serial in a women's magazine; and indeed it is in the women's magazines that Mrs. Wharton's novels now begin first to appear. *A Son
at the Front* is a little better, because it had been begun in 1918
and had her war experience in it, with some of her characteristic
cutting satire at the expense of the belligerents behind the lines. It
is not bad as a picture of the emotions of a middle-aged civilian
during the war—though not so good as Arnold Bennett's *The Pretty
Lady.*

Old New York was a much feebler second boiling from the tea-
leaves of *The Age of Innocence.* I have read only one of Mrs.
Wharton's novels written since *Old New York*: *Twilight Sleep* is
not so bad as her worst, but suffers seriously as a picture of New
York during the middle 1920's from the author's long absence
abroad. Mrs. Wharton is no longer up on her American interior-

decorating—though there are some characteristic passages of land-scape-gardening:

> "Seventy-five thousand bulbs this year!" she thought as the motor swept by the sculptured gateway, just giving and withdrawing a flash of turf sheeted with amber and lilac, in a setting of twisted and scalloped evergreens.

The two other books that I have read since then—*The Writing of Fiction* (which does, however, contain an excellent essay on Proust) and the volume of memoirs called *A Backward Glance*—I found rather disappointing. The backward glance is an exceed-ingly fleeting one which dwells very little on anything except the figure of Henry James, of whom Mrs. Wharton has left a portrait entertaining but slightly catty and curiously superficial. About her-self she tells us nothing much of interest; and she makes amends to her New York antecedents for her satire of *The Age of Innocence* by presenting them in tinted miniatures, prettily remote and unreal. It is the last irony of *The Age of Innocence* that Newland Archer should become reconciled to "old New York." "After all," he eventually came to tell himself, "there was good in the old ways." Something like this seems to have happened to Edith Wharton. Even in *A Backward Glance,* she confesses that "the weakness of the social structure" of her parents' generation had been "a blind dread of innovation"; but her later works show a dismay and a shrinking before what seemed to her the social and moral chaos of an age which was battering down the old edifice that she herself had once depicted as a prison. Perhaps, after all, the old mismated couples who had stayed married in deference to the decencies were better than the new divorced who were not aware of any duties at all.

The only thing that does survive in *A Backward Glance* is some trace of the tremendous blue-stocking that Mrs. Wharton was in her prime. The deep reverence for the heroes of art and thought —though she always believed that Paul Bourget was one of them, of the woman who in earlier days had written a long blank-verse poem about Vesalius, still makes itself felt in these memoirs. Her culture was rather heavy and grand—a preponderance of Goethe and Schiller, Racine and La Bruyère—but it was remarkably solid for an American woman and intimately related to her life. And she was one of the few Americans of her day who cared enough about serious literature to take the risks of trying to make some contribution to it. Professor Charles Eliot Norton—who had, as she dryly remarks, so admirably translated Dante—once warned her that "no great work of the imagination" had "ever been based on illicit passion." Though she herself in her later years was reduced to contemptuous complaints that the writers of the new generations had "abandoned creative art for pathology," she did have the right to insist that she had "fought hard" in her earlier days "to turn the wooden dolls" of conventional fiction "into struggling, suffering human beings." She had been one of the few such human beings in the America of the early 1900's who found an articulate voice and set down a durable record.

The above was written in 1937. An unfinished novel by Edith Wharton was published in 1938. This story, *The Buccaneers,* deserves a word of postscript. The latter part of it, even allowing for the fact that it was left in the form of a first draft, seems banal and even a little trashy. Here as elsewhere the mellowness of Mrs. Wharton's last years has dulled the sharp outlines of her fiction: there are passages in *The Buccaneers* which read like an old-fashioned story for girls. But the first section has a certain brilliance. The figures of the children of the nouveaux riches at Saratoga during the Seventies, when the post-Civil War fortunes were rolling up, come back rather diminished in memory but in lively and charming colors, like the slides of those old magic lanterns that are mentioned as one of their forms of entertainment. And we learn from Mrs. Wharton's scenario for the unfinished part of the tale that it was to have had rather an interesting development. She has here more or less reversed the values of the embittered *The Custom of the Country*: instead of playing off the culture and tradition of Europe against the vulgar Americans who are insensible to them, she dramatizes the climbing young ladies as an air-clearing and revivifying force. In the last pages she lived to write she made it plain that the hard-boiled commercial elements on the rise in both civilizations were to come to understand one another perfectly. But there is also an Anglo-Italian woman, the child of Italian revolutionaries and a cousin of Dante Gabriel Rossetti, who has been reduced to working as a governess and who has helped to engineer the success of the American girls in London. The best of these girls has been married to a dreary English duke, who represents everything least human in the English aristocratic system. Laura Testvalley was to forfeit her own hopes of capturing an amateur esthete of the older generation of the nobility in order to allow the young American to elope with an enterprising young Englishman; and thus to have let herself in for the fate of spending the rest of her days in the poverty and dullness of her home, where the old revolution had died. As the light of Edith Wharton's art grows dim and at last goes out, she leaves us, to linger on our retina, the large dark eyes of the clever spinster, the serious and attentive governess, who trades in worldly values but manages to rebuff these values; who, in following a destiny of solitude and discipline, contends for the rights of the heart; and who, child of a political movement played out, yet passes on something of its impetus to the emergence of the society of the future.

Edith Wharton and Her New Yorks

by Louis Auchincloss

The correspondence, and, no doubt, the conversations between Henry James and Edith Wharton, were carried on in the happy tone of hyperbole. It was the pose of each to appear to grovel obsequiously before the other's superiority. She professed to regard him as the master of her art, the wise, benignant guide and mentor, while he likened her to a golden eagle with a beautiful genius for great globe adventures, at whose side he was nothing but "a poor old croaking barnyard fowl." "I have simply lain stretched," he wrote her, on hearing of a motor trip in Tunisia, "a faithful old veteran slave, upon the door-mat of your palace of adventure." Yet, as is often the case in such relationships, beneath the elaborate encomiums lay a vein of hidden mockery, almost, at times, of smugness. He really thought that she was dissipating her energy and talents, while she never doubted that he was hoarding his. And neither appreciated the other's best work.

She found his later novels "more and more lacking in atmosphere, more and more severed from that thick nourishing human air in which we all live and move." Everything in them had to be fitted into a predestined design, and design, to Edith Wharton, was "one of the least important things in fiction." James, on the other hand, found her at her best when most under his influence, and considered her finest work that mild little tale, *The Reef*, where a group of sensitive, cultivated expatriates in a French chateau are reduced to quiet desperation by the discovery that one of them has had an affair with the governess. There are passages that read like a parody of James himself:

> "I want to say—Owen, you've been admirable all through."
> He broke into a laugh in which the odd elder-brotherly note was once more perceptible.
> "Admirable," she emphasized. "And so has *she*."
> "Oh, and so have you to *her!*" His voice broke down to boyishness.

Yet the master found it all of a "psychological Racinian unity, intensity, and gracility." The only thing that he questioned was why the characters, all American, should have elected to have their story carried out in France, and he warned her of the dangers of living abroad, with a wry little touch of humor at his own expense:

> Your only drawback is not having the homeliness and the inevitability and the happy limitation and the affluent poverty, of a Country of your Own (*comme moi, par exemple*)!

It was not the first time that he had sounded this warning. Ten years earlier, in 1902, he had written to her sister-in-law that she should be "tethered in native pastures, even if it reduces her to a backyard in New York." Viewed from the vantage point of today, with all of Mrs. Wharton's later novels before us that James never saw, the danger against which he warned her seems painfully obvious. It is difficult to read those slick satires about an America that she rarely bothered to visit without reflecting that she appeared, at the end, to have lost not only her country but her talent. What is curious, therefore, is that James should have foreseen this so clearly and yet should not have fully appreciated how much in 1902, and even as late as 1912, she still *had* a country, or at least a city, of her own. He may have been too out of touch with New York to appreciate how much she still belonged to it. Her ties, of course, were stronger than his. She had been brought up in the city and had married there. She had experienced its social life, in greater doses than she had wanted. She knew its men and women of property; she knew their history and their origins, their prejudices and ideals, the source of their money and how they spent their summers. This knowledge, of course, was eventually to fade with her continued residence abroad, but the ten years that preceded the first war were actually the years when her American impressions were at their most vivid and when she was doing her strongest work. It was the period of *The House of Mirth* and *The Custom of the Country,* the period when, true to her own vocation, she became the interpreter of certain aspects of New York life that she was uniquely qualified to describe.

The thing that was going on in Mrs. Wharton's New York of this period, and which she chose as the subject of her main study, was the assault upon an old and conservative group by the multitudes enriched, and fabulously enriched, by the business expansion of the preceding decades. The New York of the preassault era was the New York that she was later and nostalgically to describe in *The Age of Innocence,* the town of sober brownstone houses with high stoops, of an Academy of Music with shabby red and gold boxes, of long midday lunches with Madeira, of husbands who never went "downtown," of a sense of precedence that was military in its strictness. As she tells us in her autobiography, when her grandmother's carriage appeared on Fifth Avenue those of her aunts maintained their proper distance in the rear. To this New York belong such of her characters as Mrs. Peniston, Lawrence Selden, the Peytons, the Dagonets, the Marvells, the van der Luydens. It was a city that was worldly beyond a doubt, but worldly with a sense of order and form, with plenty of leisure time in which art, music, and literature could play a moderated role. The people from this world may lack strength of character, but their inertia is coupled with taste and observation, as seen in Lawrence Selden's parents:

> Neither one of the couple cared for money, but their disdain of it took the form of always spending a little more than was prudent. If their house was shabby, it was exquisitely kept; if there were good books on the shelves there were also good dishes on the table. Selden senior had an eye for a picture, his wife an understanding of old lace; and both were so conscious of restraint and discrimination in buying that they never quite knew how it was that the bills mounted up.

The young men practice law in a listless sort of way with much time for dining at clubs and trips to Europe. They have a settled sense of how their lives are to be led and no idea of impending change. The change, if change it really is, comes with the infiltration of the other protagonists of the drama, the Spraggs, the Wellington Brys, the Gormers, Sim Rosedale, the van Osburghs, people who can spend a thousand dollars to Mrs. Peniston's one. Their assault on the brownstone citadel of old New York and its rapid capitulation provide a study of conflicting and ultimately reconciled types of snobbishness. The reconciliation is not altogether a surprise, for snobs *can* usually be reconciled. The old society may have had a brittle and varnished shell, but it covered a materialism as rampant as that of the richest parvenu. It could only be a matter of time before the new money was made to feel at home. Mrs. Wharton anticipated Proustian distinctions in her analysis of the different layers of the social hierarchy, but it is a dreary picture unrelieved by a Swann or a Charlus. From the top to the bottom of *The House of Mirth,* from Judy Trenor and "Bellomont," down through the pushing Brys and the false bohemianism of Mattie Gormer, to the "vast, gilded" hotel life of Norma Hatch, the entire fabric revolves around money.

Conflict is lost in fusion, which brings us to the deeper drama of *The House of Mirth,* the drama not of rival classes who drown their feud in noisy merger, but of their victims, those poor beings who are weak enough to care for the luxury, but too squeamish to play the game as roughly as it must be played. Lily Bart, of course, is the most famous of these. We see her first at the age of twenty-nine, beautiful, vivid but tired, regaining behind a veil that "purity of tint" that she is beginning to lose "after years of late hours and indefatigable dancing," waiting in Grand Central "in the act of transition between one and another of the country houses that disputed her presence at the close of the Newport season." But we are soon made aware of the sea of unpaid bills and small favors in which she precariously floats. Lily suffers from the paralysis of inertia. It is not that she is unaware of the void that gapes before her; it is rather that she has too much delicacy and sensitivity, that she is too much of a lady to make the kind of marriage that will save her from the fate of turning gradually from a guest into a hanger-on. Her father has been of old New York, but her mother, one gathers, is of more ordinary material, and it has been the

latter's greed that has driven him to make the fortune that he is
bound, by the same web of fate that enmeshes his daughter, to lose.
So Lily is of both worlds; she understands both, and, before she
has done, she has slipped between them and fallen prostrate beneath their stamping feet. The pathos of her fall is that the failure
to act which precipitates each stage of her descent does not come
from any superiority of moral resolution but rather from a refinement of taste, a fastidiousness, of which neither her meticulous
aunt, Mrs. Peniston, nor her coarse admirer, Mr. Rosedale, have
the remotest understanding. Indeed, one feels that Lily Bart, in all
New York, is the lone and solitary lady. Yet with each slip in the
ladder she experiences the coarsening that comes with the increased
sense of the necessity of holding on, and though she can never bring
herself to tell George Dorset of his wife's infidelity, even to win the
town's richest husband and triumph over her most vindictive
opponent, she can ultimately face the prospect of marriage with Sim
Rosedale as a way of getting the money to pay a debt of honor.
And when she does stoop it is too late; even Sim Rosedale won't
have her, and Lily takes the final drop to the milliner's shop and
ultimately to the overdose of sleeping tablets.

In *The Custom of the Country* Mrs. Wharton is again dealing
with the conflict of materialisms, but this time the central study is
of a parvenu, Undine Spragg, who cuts her way to the top of the
heap. Her victim—for there is always a victim—is a man. Ralph
Marvell is self-consciously of "aboriginal New York"; his forebears
whose tradition he can never forget have been "small, cautious,
middle-class" in their ideals, with "a tranquil disdain for money-
getting" and "a passive openness to the finer sensations." But Ralph
has just enough curiosity to be interested in "the invaders," as he
calls the new rich; with cultivated decadence he finds an essential
simplicity in their acquisitiveness. His cousin, Clare, another victim,
has married invader Peter Van Degen and learned to repent, "but
she repented in the Van Degen diamonds, and the Van Degen motor
bore her broken heart from opera to ball." Ralph sees it all clearly,
but he is to be different. He is to save the "innocence" of the
Spraggs; he is to keep *them* from corruption. He goes down to speedy
ruin before Undine, and his suicide is almost a matter of course.
The victim, however, is too naïve; one's sympathy is confounded

with impatience. It is Undine's book; her victims are incidental. She is the personification of the newcomer, absolutely vulgar and absolutely ruthless. Everything happens to Undine, but nothing affects her. She marries once for money, a second time for family and a third time for money again, only to find in the end that her divorces will keep her from being an ambassadress. And that, of course, is the only thing that she ultimately wants.

The Custom of the Country appeared in 1913, and the next four years Mrs. Wharton devoted entirely to war work. Her main job was with the Red Cross in Paris, but she visited military hospitals at the front and from a cottage garden at Clermont-en-Argonne she witnessed the victorious French assault on the heights of Vauquois. But the "fantastic heights and depths of self-devotion and ardor, of pessimism, triviality, and selfishness," as she describes the war years, did little more for her as a writer than they have done, in either war, for many others. Their most important effect was to introduce a note of nostalgia, an escape, as she describes it, to childhood memories of a long-vanished America, to the "mild blur of rosy and white-whiskered gentlemen, of ladies with bare sloping shoulders rising flower-like from voluminous skirts, peeped at from the stair-top while wraps were removed in the hall below." But this was the New York, was it not, that she had found so stuffy and confining, that she had shown in losing battle with the Spraggs and Rosedales and from which she had fled to Europe? It was a New York, was it not, that had been passive, inert, confining, a city that had almost deserved to be eaten up by the new money of the energetic parvenu? Now, however, that it was gone, really gone, she found herself looking about and wondering if she had not gone too far in its condemnation. Much later she was to confess:

> When I was young it used to seem to me that the group in which I grew up was like an empty vessel into which no new wine would ever again be poured. Now I see that one of its uses lay in preserving a few drops of an old vintage too rare to be savored by a youthful palate.

Out of this sense of apology came *The Age of Innocence*. It deals with a New York that is pre-Spragg and pre-Rosedale. Newland Archer is the young Whartonian of brownstone lineage, the Marvell type, a lawyer, of course, with a leisurely practice and an eye for books and pictures. He marries conventionally, and the story of the book is that he does *not* leave his wife to go off with the Countess Olenska, New York-born but emancipated. There is no feeling, however, that Archer has condemned himself and the Countess to an unrewarding life of frustration. The author is absorbed in the beauty of rules and forms even when they stamp out spontaneity. "It was you," the Countess tells Archer, "who made me understand that under the dullness there are things so fine and sensitive and delicate that even those I most cared for in my other life look cheap in comparison." This is the climax of the message: that under the thick glass of convention blooms the fine, fragile flower of patient suffering and denial. To drop out of society is as vulgar as to predominate; one must endure and properly smile.

The novel, however, despite its note of calm resignation and sacrifice, is pervaded with a sense of materialism. The presence of "things" clogs even the best of Mrs. Wharton's writing. The author of *The House of Mirth* was also the author of *The Decoration of Houses*. One feels the charm of Ellen Olenska, but one feels it too much in her taste and possessions: "some small slender tables of dark wood, a delicate little Greek bronze in the chimney piece, and a stretch of red damask nailed on the discolored wallpaper behind a couple of Italian-looking pictures in old frames." She has "only two" Jacqueminot roses in a slender vase, and her tea is served "with handleless Japanese cups and little covered dishes." She finds a friend in Philistia; he understands Europe, and their refuge is in the arts, but their talk is filled with references to private rooms at Delmonico's and "little oyster suppers." Even in her moment of greatest emotional strain, when she looks at her watch she looks at a "little gold-faced watch on an enameled chain." The vigor of the earlier books is largely gone, but the sense of the world remains.

It was now that Edith Wharton found herself at the crossroads. She could have continued in the nostalgic vein of *The Age of Innocence* and tethered herself, in James's phrase, to the native pastures of her early memories. The tendency might have been toward the sentimental, but the result could have had the charm of remembered things. One can see this in the little series known as *Old New York*.

But, unfortunately, she chose for her major efforts the contemporary scene, especially the American scene, although it was a decade since she had crossed the Atlantic to revisit her native shores. Older and shriller, she denounced the vulgarity that she was now beginning to find in everything, judging America, the country in her eyes most responsible, by the standards of Riviera expatriates whom she did not even know.

The vulgarity on which she had declared war ended by overwhelming her novels. Taste, the chosen guide of her later years, went back on her. In the final dissolution, as with the Barts and Rosedales, conflict is again lost in merger. The very titles of the later books betray the drop of her standards; they are flat and ugly: *Human Nature, The Mother's Recompense, Twilight Sleep, The Glimpses of the Moon.* The caricature of American life becomes grotesque. The towns are given names like Delos, Aeschylus, Lohengrin, or Halleluja, and the characters speak an anglicized dialect full of such terms as "Hang it!" "Chuck it!" "He's a jolly chap," and "A fellow needs. . . ." The town slogan of Euphoria in *Hudson River Bracketed* is "Me for the front row." And the American face! How it haunts her! It is "as unexpressive as a football"; it might have been made by "a manufacturer of sporting goods." Its sameness encompasses her "with its innocent uniformity." How many of such faces would it take "to make up a single individuality"? And, ironically enough, as her indignation mounts her style loses its old precision and begins to take on the slickness of a popular magazine story. Compare, for example, these two descriptions of a lady on the threshold of a European hotel. The first is from *Madame de Treymes,* written in 1907, one of her Jamesian passages, but highly polished:

> The mere fact of her having forgotten to draw on her gloves as they were descending in the hotel lift from his mother's drawing room was, in this connection, charged with significance to Durham. She was the kind of woman who always presents herself to the mind's eye as completely equipped, as made of exquisitely cared for and finely related details; and that the heat of her parting with his family should have left her unconscious that she was emerging gloveless into Paris seemed, on the whole, to speak hopefully for Durham's future opinion of the city. Even now, he could detect a certain confusion, a

desire to draw breath and catch up with her life, in the way she
dawdled over the last buttons in the dimness of the porte-cochère,
while her footman, outside, hung on her retarded signal.

The second is from *The Glimpses of the Moon,* fifteen years later:

> But on the threshold a still more familiar figure met her: that of a
> lady in exaggerated pearls and sables, descending from an exaggerated
> motor, like the motors in magazine advertisements, the huge arks in
> which jeweled beauties and slender youths pause to gaze at snow peaks
> from an Alpine summit.

Specimens of old New York in the novels now become spindly
and ridiculous, like Mr. Wyant in *Twilight Sleep* and Mr. Spears
in *Hudson River Bracketed.* The Wheaters in *The Children* are
meant to be rich New Yorkers traveling in Europe. Their children,
of various nationalities, their absurd marital mix-up, their impossible, red-carpeted, be-yachted life, with a movie star ex-wife whose
favorite swear word is "Fudge!" and an American-born princess who
hopes that the size of families will be regulated by legislation, con-
stitute a grotesque parody of international drifters. Mrs. Wharton
has no true insight into their lives; she stands apart like her spokesman, Mrs. Sellars, in disdain, describing the Wheaters only in terms
of snobbish and disapproving suppositions.

Eventually there seemed to be no aspect of American life that
did not disgust her. It was not only the vulgar rich; there were also
the vulgar intellectuals. This passage from *The Gods Arrive* is
meant to represent a conversation between young American writers
in Paris:

> "Poor old Fynes," another of them took it up, "sounded as if he'd
> struck a new note because he made his people talk in the vernacular.
> Nothing else new about *him*—might have worked up his method out
> of Zola. Probably did."
> "Zola—who's he?" somebody yawned.
> "Oh, I dunno. The French Thackeray, I guess."
> "See here, fellows, who's read Thackeray, anyhow?"
> "Nobody since Lytton Strachey, I guess."
> "Well, anyway, *This Globe* is one great big book. Eh, Vance, that
> the way you see it?"

Vance roused himself and looked at the speaker. "Not the way I see life. Life's continuous!"

"Life continuous—continuous? Why, it's a series of jumps in the dark. That's Mendel's law, anyhow," another budding critic took up the argument.

"Gee! Who's Mendel? Another new novelist?"

The meeting between Mrs. Wharton and Scott Fitzgerald, as described by Arthur Mizener, is symptomatic of her uneasy relationships with the younger generation of writers. She found him crude, and he found her stiff and superior. But behind his sophomoric urge to shock a strait-laced old lady, lurked intense admiration and curiosity. He confessed once, half seriously, to Margaret Chanler that he had three ambitions in life: to write the best and clearest prose of the twentieth century, to remain faithful to Zelda, and to become an intimate friend of Mrs. Wharton. Mrs. Chanler's response was the same that her friend Edith might have made: "As to your first ambition, I hope you attain it. As to your second, it is too personal for me to comment on. But as to your third, young man, you'll have to cut down your drinking!"

As with so many who seem proud and stiff, Mrs. Wharton's real trouble lay in shyness. She described it to Adèle Burden as the "dread disease" that had martyrized her in youth. She had finally come to terms with the world of her contemporaries, and it may have seemed too much to have to fight that battle with a new generation. She resented the formlessness of a world that seemed to have repudiated the very formalities that she had once satirized. When *The Mother's Recompense* was misunderstood by critics, she was deeply discouraged by the "densities of comprehension" that surrounded her. She wrote to Mrs. Chanler:

> You will wonder that the priestess of the life of reason should take such things to heart, and I wonder too. I never have minded before, but as my work reaches its close, I feel so sure that it is either nothing, or far more than they know. And I wonder, a little desolately, which?

In 1937, the year in which she died, Mrs. Wharton was working on a novel that shows a brief, renewed interest in the New York of her childhood from which she drew *The Age of Innocence*. This is

the posthumously published fragment, *The Buccaneers,* the unfinished story of three American girls in the Seventies who make
brilliant English marriages and become the envy of a New York
which had scorned them. The book has more life than its immediate predecessors, but on its very opening page we find its author
still laying on satire at the expense of America with the now customary trowel. She refers to certain tall white columns on the portico
of the Grand Union Hotel in Saratoga which "so often reminded
cultured travelers of the Parthenon at Athens (Greece)."

Guy Thwarte in this unfinished tale is the thread that links it with
so many of its predecessors. Although English, he is still the
Wharton hero, tall and good-looking, a Gibson man, and, to the
amazement of his family, though he has a "decent reputation about
women" and is a "brilliant point-to-point rider," he "messes about"
with poetry and painting. Like the heroes of French classic tragedy
the Wharton men keep their action off stage. Guy consents to dip
into commerce, but only in foreign climes. He disappears to Brazil
for four years and returns a millionaire, but the "dark, rich, stormy
years of his exile" lie "like a raging channel between himself and
his old life." The notes at the end of the book show that he was
fated to elope with the Duchess of Tintagel; it was to be the triumph
of "love, deep and abiding love." One cannot feel after this any
keen regret that the story was never finished. Lily Bart's love for
Lawrence Selden is the one hollow note of *The House of Mirth.*
Undine Spragg in *The Custom of the Country* is, of course, incapable of love. Love in *The Age of Innocence* is stifled by the
characters themselves. Mrs. Wharton at her best was an analyst of
the paralysis that attends failure in the market place and of the
coarseness that attends success. Hers was not a world where romance
was apt to flourish.

The Novels of Edith Wharton

by Percy Lubbock

Mrs. Wharton's books, from the earliest to the latest, are more than a collection of penetrating and finely finished studies; they are linked episodes in one continuous adventure, the adventure of her rare and distinguished critical intelligence. She is a writer who has never, so to say, relapsed into a settled life. As an artist she seems to have cared little, perhaps she has not cared enough, to sit still and receive impressions passively. Her choice has been less to watch the drifting images than to seize and to question them. She has waylaid all manner of dramatic moments in widely various scenes, not merely in different lands under different skies, but in a large diversity of mental and moral climates. She has made many experiments, and has been drawn aside into not a few digressions, some of which have seemed to break, a little too abruptly, the forward march of her work. Yet her restless movement has never been wayward, for it has been directed by a single intention; and it is precisely this that has brought her work to the brilliance it has latterly reached, not merely of lucidity and precision, but of quick color and expressive charm. Her intention has clearly been to leave no image and no moment uncriticized, to analyze every impression and to interrogate every conclusion; and the timely moral pointed by her work is the dependence of the reason and beauty of literary form upon this activity.

Mrs. Wharton, then, seizing her material, the treasure of an unwritten story or study or novel, has shown that the way to begin is to rend the precious stuff in pieces. The meaning of the delight which an artist finds in this initial process is plentifully misunder-

"The Novels of Edith Wharton" by Percy Lubbock. From *The Quarterly Review*, January 1915. Reprinted by permission of Hope Leresche & Steele.

stood. The blade of analysis is commonly regarded as destructive; and the writer who rejoices in its use as openly as the author of Mrs. Wharton's earlier volumes is certain to be taxed, if not with mere malice, at least with the failure to discern the warm penumbra of humanity which envelops beauty with its most appealing grace. It would be far more reasonable to measure the force with which the grace has been felt by this determination to insulate and lay bare its elements. The writer well knows the object and the possible reward of his violence. The treasure is torn to bits in the knowledge that it will presently redispose itself ideally. It will strain towards the right shape, the shape that the haphazard chances of life had prevented it from assuming. Rescued at last from the accidental and the alien, the unwritten book begins to find its form. Its essential germ, whatever it may be, is one and unique. Its unity may be that of a figure, a life, a vista of circumstance, a set of relations—in any case it is indivisible; and as soon as it is extricated it expands anew and is ready for its full and logical expression. This at least is its response in the mind of the novelist, the mind in which an infused idea becomes, not an argument, but an acted drama on a set stage. In another mind the flowering and fruiting of the idea, though not less lively, will be different. There is a seed of indestructible fertility in anything that has really been understood, and if its growth is secret, there is nothing mysterious about the manner in which it is induced to branch.

Thus it is that, looking back from Mrs. Wharton's later command of large and intricate design, we may recognize it as the direct result of an incessantly inquisitive criticism. Her earlier and shorter pieces are like a series of serried question marks, each confronting some selected case or moment of life, every one of which is called upon to stop and explain, in the fewest words, its precise significance. Its significance, accordingly, dictates the fashion and the scope of the small drama; and, as the author's hand grows more and more assured, so the chosen themes, the moments detained in their flight, begin to make more elaborate and difficult claims. The readiness to put questions is not always the same, it must be conceded, as the readiness to wait for answers; and, as to that, we may sometimes find that this insatiable interrogator darts ahead of her subject, at a pace faster than any at which life can respond. Life, it is true, will move on the whole as fast as we please; but, though it reacts to the acute question with delight, it cannot be expected to summarize its answer in a flash, and at times the space of a flash seems to be all it gets from Mrs. Wharton. Her difficulty here is simply the extraordinary ease with which she discovers fresh problems to be elucidated. There is one gift we could occasionally wish for her, and that is the gift of forgetting that there are more picturesque chances and incidents in the world than one—the one for the moment under our eyes. As it is, she now and then seems, in her earlier volumes, to dismiss her story while it is still asking for a further hearing; not because she can get no more out of it, but because of the other clamorous stories awaiting their turns.

At the same time, if Mrs. Wharton's touch, in some of her books, has been unduly light, another explanation is discoverable. Almost invariably she has used the short story for the comedy of irony, to which indeed the short story more particularly lends itself. Her odd cases, queer motives, awkward episodes, have generally been such as displayed themselves in that particular light. Now there is nothing in the world which irony so much and so rightly fears as overemphasis. It has a horror of blackening the telling line or of carrying the expressive gesture too far; and, in recoiling from that excess, it may easily make the more sophisticated mistake of not carrying it far enough. Moreover irony, though it works without a qualm or a doubt in the comedy of situation, can never be quite so sure of itself where it is called upon to irradiate the portrait of a character. Situations, conjunctions of human beings, are more definite and controllable than human beings themselves; and, where but few resources of character are called into play by the action, irony can keep it in hand without difficulty. Character itself, character directly faced and studied, more readily eludes it.

The titular piece in the volume called *The Descent of Man* is an instance to the point. A serious but all too adaptable man of science happens upon certain books of a familiar sort, books which have won an immense popular success by their exploitation of the yearnings of an uncritical public for something it can regard as scientific and philosophical, without danger to its intellectual complacency. The professor amuses himself with the ironical production of a book of this kind. The immediate issue is obvious: the professor's irony will be so fine that it will not prevent his book from obtaining precisely the same success as the effusions he set out to parody, the author himself falling thereby for the first time under the spell of popularity and its rewards. We wait to see what further and rarer stroke Mrs. Wharton has in store for us. But no: she will not prolong a matter which, given the lively and sensitive consciousness of the professor, we feel would have gone further. With the amount of character she has given him (and the situation required no less) he would no doubt have had more to say.

On the other hand, to take an instance from the same volume, the story called "The Other Two" sows its small circle perfectly described. Here again there is no surprise for the reader, for we see from the first that the climax is to be the embarrassing assembly, round her tea-table, of Mrs. Waythorn's three husbands, the one in present possession and his two discarded predecessors. But here Mrs. Wharton's question, still to call it so, is a simple one. She starts no problem of character and of the effect on it of circumstances, as in the case of the professor. She simply asks: What would such a scene be like?—and evokes the neatest and completest of answers. So too in the matchless "Mission of Jane," where a disaffected couple are finally united in tenderness by their common, but scrupulously unspoken, dislike of their terrible adopted daughter, the thing is conceived, not as an adventure in psychology, but as an incident to be viewed in one long glance of amusement. To this class belong the happiest of these stories, such as "The Rembrandt," "The Pelican," "The Angel at the Grave," in all of which the men and women, hapless and perplexed as they are, arise directly from their own histories. Their histories preceded them, and they have only to act them out. Where Mrs. Wharton has reversed the process and found her drama by exploring minds and characters of a certain cast ("The Recovery," "The Moving Finger," "A Coward," to name some examples), the scene is apt to result less fortunately. Character, of the sort that requires for its exhibition no more room than the miniature stage of some twenty pages, is obviously character closely pruned, character rigorously simplified for the sake of a single dominant feature. On these terms its movement, in such pieces as those just mentioned, appears both a little constrained and a little vague, as though it were still conscious of the sacrifice, in variety of temperament and interest, which it has been called on to make. Mrs. Wharton, in short, has succeeded better in transposing groups of people, concatenations of incident, into the key of the short story, than in doing the like with the looser agglomeration of the human mind.

The inference to be drawn is evident. If character, so summarized and foreshortened, seemed inclined to be unmanageable, it was tacitly asking to be treated on a larger scale. It was asking, that is to say, for the opportunity of acting and reacting against its like, of showing the stuff of which it is made by confronting other moving and living forces. The opportunity for this is the opportunity for the novel. The short story is the breaking of a wave upon a fixed rock; it cannot perhaps treat the subject which shows a reciprocal clash, the shock of two meeting waves. If this is so, it would be natural that a writer of Mrs. Wharton's speculative and critical imagination should not readily regard the world as a motionless foil for the display of a single impulse. She would rather watch the difficult and highly modern minds which interest her, in their more or less embarrassed conflicts with each other and with the living world of manners. In other words, she would write novels; and in fact it is in her novels that her work has reached its ripeness. Of these the actual first lies outside the line to be followed here. *The Valley of Decision* was of the nature of an experiment by the way, and excursion into what is called "historical" fiction. It was an experiment which in such hands could not be uninteresting, though its sedulous avoidance of the commonplace note of romance does not quite secure it against occasional theatricality. But as a curious and careful study of the Italy of the eighteenth century it demands a different sort of criticism. From the point of view adopted in these pages it is *The House of Mirth* which ranks as Mrs. Wharton's first novel.

The breadth and the fullness of this book are doubly remarkable. In the first place, in spite of a certain flaw in the structure, to be mentioned presently, there is no sort of constraint about the execution. It is handled with straightforward freedom, and makes its points with evenness and clarity. But *The House of Mirth* also takes us at a stride into the question, hardly raised by its predecessors, of the social and organized (or antisocial and disorganized) life which

Mrs. Wharton now proceeded to use for her purposes. America, in fact, and in particular New York, appears as it had not yet appeared in her work. The "crucial instances" of her earlier books were not, on the whole, specifically American. They were types of some of the difficulties to which the victims of modernity are heirs, wherever among modern conditions their lot may happen to have been cast. Many of them, no doubt, were naturally rooted in American soil, but in these America is merely an assumed background, conditioning the action without taking part in it. In *The House of Mirth* New York is no background; it is an urgent and voluble participator in the drama. It is an actor, indeed, so vehemently alive that Mrs. Wharton's easy and immediate control of such exuberance is a triumph of stage-management. *The House of Mirth* is thoroughly the novel of a novelist; it shows, that is to say, no sign whatever that its author had been accustomed to find her subjects in momentary glimpses that did not ask for broader development. She refocuses her sight, apparently without effort, to include one of the most remarkable spectacles in the history of manners—the sudden unfolding of a social growth fertilized by vaster streams of private wealth than the world has ever yet known. The glittering show which we associate with the name of Fifth Avenue may, for the service of art, leave something to be desired. But its very intractability is so vividly marked, in a world in which social definitions are everywhere becoming vaguer, that it clearly challenges art to the attempt to make use of it.

The evident difficulty is that the growth has been too sudden to strike us as organic. A living society, as we understand the word, can draw its being only from a stored inheritance of traditions; and the leading feature of this particular New York is its freedom from any discernible debt to the past. This, no doubt, is a superficial view of the matter, for we are presumably not prepared to regard the millionaire as a miraculous and unrelated species. The millionaire and his hierarchy have had their own origins; and evolution is not the less natural for being rapid. The structure of this singular House of Mirth is therefore no more meaningless than any other; and the novelist who could expound its meaning by showing the continuity which it must have with its mysterious past would have a brilliant subject to his hand. Unfortunately the novelist, as things are, is scarcely in a position to do this, cut off as his experience is likely to be from the conditions of life which have brought about these huge accumulations. He cannot see the new society as the inevitable outcome of ancestral forces, for the necessary links lie in a region which it is usually forbidden him to tread, the region densely veiled from him under the name of "business." Till that veil is rent he must chiefly be struck by the passion with which this society has flung itself into the attempt to buy everything that can be bought, and its amazing success in doing so. For the romance of expenditure this is all very well, but the novel of manners looks for something more coherent. No picture could be made of a promiscuity which streams beyond the limits of any frame that might be imposed upon it. A writer like Mrs. Wharton, who touches nothing but to give it finality, could treat Fifth Avenue's indiscriminate raptures in only one way. Her Trenors and Dorsets and van Degens, scattering their millions on both sides of the Atlantic, do not and could not give her a subject for direct study; but it is a different matter when she annexes and uses them for particular issues. If it is difficult to see what they mean or how they were created, what they are devouring or supplanting is less obscure. Mrs. Wharton accordingly pictures, not the Trenors themselves, but their disturbing impact upon other and more impressionable surfaces.

In *The House of Mirth* it is Lily Bart whom they devour, or rather whom they so mold and train that when, by what might have been the fortune of her life, they cease to find a use for her, she can only drop helpless by the way. Lily's fineness of grain, her central independence of spirit, perpetually prevent her from harvesting the profit which her cultivation of the Trenors and their like brings under her hand. The fruits of her dependence have a certain grossness of texture which always makes her, when choice has to be made, neglect to appropriate them. She pays for her fastidiousness by finding herself abandoned by the vivid crowd; and she pays for her courtship of the crowd, so carefully taught her by nearly all the conditions of her life, by discovering that her independence is only strong enough to destroy and not to remake her. In the wavering drama of Lily's hesitations her independence is represented by the one friend who is both near enough to affect her and critical enough to have kept himself free on his own ground. Selden knows, and she

knows, that if she is to create an existence of finer values for herself
it can be only with his help. Yet between them they fail; and Lily,
cast off at last by the crowd for her failure to treat with them consistently on their own terms, does not, at the moment of need, find
the outstretched hand. So her drama must necessarily end; for, in the
middle of a world which with all accuracy knows what it wants, there
is no time for hesitation to feel its way and grow tentatively into
strength. This we can easily recognize; but Mrs. Wharton appears,
in arranging her effects, to have assumed a little too much for the
pace and stress of the hurrying world. That Lily must drop out is
clear; and doubtless her subsidence would be rapid. But that her
disappearance into obscurity should seem so little remarked, that
she should vanish without more splash, is difficult to reconcile with
the conspicuousness of her preceding triumphs, especially as her
reluctant exile is no further in space than from the palaces of one
street to the boarding-houses of the next. We feel that it would take
even the Trenors more time than Mrs. Wharton allows them to
ignore Lily so completely, with the splendor of her beauty languish-
ing within five minutes' walk. If this only means that we do not
know the race of Trenors as Mrs. Wharton knows them—which
indeed is likely—there was then all the more need to convince us
securely. But except at this one juncture there seems no detail
wanting to our knowledge of Lily's tyrannous world, so direct is
Mrs. Wharton's use of sharp descriptive strokes. Nothing could be
more unobtrusively right than the way in which the gilded crowd
surges over the picture, and parts, at the due moments, to give place
to the sensitive quiet of the scenes between Lily and Selden with
which the book is exquisitely punctuated.

In *The Custom of the Country* Mrs. Wharton has lately resumed
the question of New York for a different purpose. Here again we
have the crowd; but this time the crowd reacts, not merely against
a personal episode in its midst, but against old traditions of life
and manners which it half imitates, half defies. One such tradition,
very finely flavored if a little exhausted by age, is close at hand,
occupying the actual ground which has produced the more flam-
boyant crop. The dignity and discretion of this old New York,
it is easy to see, will be a frail protection when it is called upon to
deal with the insurgent newcomers, and it is likely enough to find

itself disconcerted. There will be an eventful story to tell when, cleaving her way through new and old alike, with a determination that grows with her growing perception of her needs, appears Undine—Undine who has emerged from the newest of all, from the resounding void of the Middle West, with her dewy loveliness and her pair of forlorn and bewildered parents. The Middle West is rich enough to float Undine to New York, but it is her unaided beauty that carries her on from that point and that scars a great disturbing track across lives as firmly rooted, as broadly civilized, as her own is unattached and unconditioned. Undine has nothing and is nothing but her beauty, with just the wit to enable her to perceive that there are worlds where noise and expense are not taken as the measure of all values. If the strongholds of secluded dignity cannot be bought, beauty such as hers can reduce them. Washington Square soon falls; and the Faubourg Saint Germain, when its turn comes later on, holds out not much longer. Undine may droop for a moment in the rarefied air of these retreats, but she easily reasserts herself. In the encounter between her futility and the concentrated significance of old fashions and old manners, it is she who slips away unscathed, possessing as she does nothing more sensitive than her beauty. It is the trained and inherited power of living and feeling that alone knows how to pay and that consequently pays the whole price. Undine is free to regard herself as misjudged and ill-treated, and to carry her undimmed radiance back again to the world she understands.

Each of Mrs. Wharton's later books has represented a new difficulty mastered, and the particular trophy of *The Custom of the Country* is not to be missed, especially when it is placed side by side with *The House of Mirth*. The story of Lily Bart, as we then see, is to the story of Undine as a tapestry unrolled to a picture painted in far-reaching aerial perspective. It is not a question of a difference in lively quality. The figures of the earlier tale are as distinct and vivid as those of the later, and their gestures are as free. The difference is that in *The Custom of the Country* they have air and light and space all round them, that as we watch them they seem able to move towards us and retreat away from us, whereas the procession of *The House of Mirth* passes across its pages at a constant distance from the spectator. The way of the procession is not necessarily, for that, an inferior way; it has its own appropriate and decorative completeness. But the fable of Undine, with its much more elaborate study in contrasts, needed a stage deep as well as wide. The shallower scene is enough for the seething rout to spend its money in; the shapely structures of a world which is openly based upon its past demand a setting in which the gradations of distance are as carefully indicated as the foreground. In _The Custom of the Country,_ for all its big sweep from continent to continent, the eye is never distracted by the flutter and flash of Undine's restlessness, for it is constantly aware of the spreading social landscape in which she ranges so irresponsibly. It is in particular the spectacle of French life, the life that is lived behind the huge-portaled housefronts in the narrow streets of the Faubourg, and the life that passes in what Mrs. Heeny, Undine's irrepressible masseuse, pleasantly calls the "Shutter country," which absorbs the gaze with its deep layers of distinction and monotony and expressive composure, of immemorial ignorance of the world coupled with the finest expertness in manipulating the fabric of existence. Its contrast at every point with Undine's inarticulate and barbaric innocence, which the ransacked spoils of a dozen climates leave exactly as blank as before, is worked out, filled in, rounded off with a precision that shows not a single touch mistimed or out of place.

The Custom of the Country, in short, is a fine book, but unluckily it is all too good for Undine. It is difficult to see, given the lines on which Mrs. Wharton has treated the action, how it could have been otherwise. Undine, as a mere bubble of rainbow tints, may possibly have substance enough to wound and destroy, though it is perhaps doubtful whether we can quite accord all that Mrs. Wharton claims for beauty so unsupported by any gifts of character whatever. At any rate, if this empty shining fairness is to be endowed with such importance, it is clear that we must be made to see it at every turn and be conscious of it at every moment. It must fill the air for us with the very same revelation of glowing light that bewitched its victims. But Mrs. Wharton for the most part chooses to look in the opposite direction; that is to say, she makes us chiefly see with Undine's eyes and watch her beauty as it is reflected in the intent gaze of her adorers. So and in no better way could we be convinced of many a vision of enchantment, but the workings of Undine's mind are altogether too rudimentary to help us out in her case. Undine, being nothing but an exquisite object, should surely have been treated exclusively as an object. This is no doubt a somewhat subversive reflection to throw out in passing, for it of course implies a point of departure and a way of approach to the story entirely different from those which Mrs. Wharton has chosen. Where in this case she could have found a controlling and unifying center is a question it might be inconvenient to tackle. But it seems as though Undine's triviality could not otherwise be made strong enough to carry the piled-up irony of her career through such a series of glittering scenes.

Mrs. Wharton has only once, outside these two novels, used America in the sense in which it is used in them. This was not when she wrote *The Fruit of the Tree,* although in fact that story never leaves American soil. There she reverted to the subject which arises out of a particular equivocal case, a case which may happen to be American but is not necessarily so. It is treated with much less assurance than Mrs. Wharton had shown in its immediate predecessor, *The House of Mirth.* She seems to fasten on her theme with some uncertainty, and in consequence to leave it both incomplete and rather diffusely amplified. But *The Fruit of the Tree* may be passed over here because it puts us in touch with a side of Mrs. Wharton's imagination which we shall presently find far more clearly and richly illuminated. Meanwhile, directly facing the full glare of the relentless American light, comes the grim little story called *Ethan Frome.* Here indeed is American life of a tougher substance than that of Fifth Avenue, life as tightly wedged in its snow-piled mountain valleys as the other drifts aimlessly. In such a setting the simplest notes fall sharply on a wintry silence which seems to be waiting for unrelieved and fantastic tragedies like Ethan's. The bitter futilities which imprison Ethan's existence close on it again faster than ever after his one crowning and vain attempt to bring passion, if not to life, at least to death. Not only is the gift of death denied to Ethan and Mattie, but they may not even live in an undesecrated memory of their single contact with beauty. By the long anticlimax of their fate memory itself is corroded; and it is the mean indignity of pain, not its sanctity, which is thrown upon Ethan's tragic powers of endurance.

There is no prescribing the limitations of a talent which never tires of the enterprise of criticism. Mrs. Wharton's art, trained on all the refinements and sophistications of modernity, rose in *Ethan Frome* to meet suggestions of an entirely new kind and instantly singled out their peculiar demand. We can see in the finished tale exactly what this demand was and how easy it would have been to overlook it. Ethan's history was just a flash of inarticulate passion, thrown against the blinding whiteness of the New England winter. There are no halftones in such a life, and nothing for the writer to do—so it might seem, but to give with as few strokes as possible the huge monotony of the snow and the brief storm of Ethan's rebellion. The story would need only the telling juxtaposition of two such intense effects. It would be a drama, but a drama of landscape, the dumbness of these village tragedies being such as to make them appear but a part, even a subordinate part, of the scene—mountain or field or forest—which witnesses them. We have had a good deal of this decorative treatment of village life, and America seems to have had still more; but we have not had much of the sort that Mrs. Wharton gives us. *Ethan Frome* is not in the least a study of genre. Its landscape is there, and there with all vividness, but it is behind it. The action in front, the strange calamitous issue, has its perfectly independent movement. It is not described for the sake of the picturesque scene; the scene is described, the snow blazes, for the sake of the action. How, then, was Ethan's story, where there is so little that can happen and so much less still that can be spoken in words, to be made to stand out and take the eye with its own dramatic value? This, as Mrs. Wharton has seen, is the appeal of the story to such art as hers, for which a mere "landscape with figures" would be too easy to be interesting. She meets the appeal in a manner more difficult to define than to recognize and admire.

What is it, in fact, which makes the slightest, most trivial incident seem, under certain hands, to glow with an inner light, to appear unique and final and incomparable with anything else, so that we do not think of weighing or measuring it by any general standard? The little characteristic episode, chosen by the novelist to illustrate some development of a situation, may become, if it has this quality, a poem of delight, where, if the quality is lacking, we are only irritated by the transparency of the novelist's art. The great master of this particular subtlety is undoubtedly Tolstoy, with his extraordinary power of absorbing the whole of our attention with a few light touches, till the scene evoked grows important and urgent, a thing to be watched breathlessly, even though it may be no more than the picture of a stable-boy saddling a horse or a child amusing itself with a box of paints. Whatever it consists in, this power is at work in *Ethan Frome*. The tiny incidents which lead gradually up to the strange catastrophe are magnetized and luminous and *quick*. We do not feel that Mrs. Wharton, in telling her story by means of such small homely events, is using a clever artistic restraint; we feel, on the contrary, that the events—a tramp through the snow, the breaking of a glass dish, the carrying of a trunk downstairs—are the natural and sufficient channels of great emotion. How is it done? The question touches what is perhaps the central and most distinguishing gift of the true novelist, his power of so completely identifying himself with the character through whose eyes he is seeing that his field of vision, both in extent and in particularity, is exactly no more and no less than that of the man or woman he has imagined. Mrs. Wharton, in the few and simple pages of *Ethan Frome*, has shown more conclusively that she possesses this power than in anything else she has written, for she has written nothing in which she has so rigorously denied herself all other help.

But all this time, though we have seen Mrs. Wharton with gathering assurance approach her task from different sides, we have not found her concentrating her whole mind upon a certain part of it which she was bound to undertake in time. The novelist's task is a complex of more or less distinguishable problems; and in any single fiction, of the kind capable of sustaining such criticism, we can point to one of them as that which the writer has had principally to treat. The problem which Mrs. Wharton at last reached in *The Reef* is that of the squarely faced, intently studied portrait; and the portrait she produced is surely on the whole the most compellingly beautiful thing in all her work. She has never been more happily at home with her material—for her material has never been of finer paste—than she appears in creating the figure of Anna Leath. Anna, indeed, gives us the sense that she had all along been waiting for Mrs. Wharton, assured that the time would come when the one person who could do her justice would be ready to take her

in hand. They were made for each other. Anna's answering light-
ness and softness and warmth vibrate instantly to Mrs. Wharton's
touch—pressure so perfectly timed in its rhythm that the movement
of hand required to exert it is barely perceptible. There are moments
in *The Reef* when it seems impossible that Anna can continue to
satisfy demands which grow ever quieter and more searching; yet
the more her capacity is taxed, the more sensitively she responds.
The security with which Mrs. Wharton is able to count on her is,
of course, the measure of what she has put into her; and this is
perhaps more than a critic, who sees Anna from our side of the
Atlantic, can hope to recognize completely. Anna is American in
every syllable of her history and to the last recesses of her consciousness—that is certain; but she is an American that represents no
antithesis to Europe. She is rather, for the most part, the affirmed
and intensified expression of just the qualities usually supposed to
be the legacy of long-settled traditions. Only an American—not to
attempt a more precise definition—could be as fragrantly, as
exquisitely, as *painfully* civilized as Anna, with her heritage of
sensibility, her anxious discriminations, her devious and shadowy
shyness. We can follow her sympathetically through all this; but
her minutely stippled discretion baffles us in the end by what we
can only call its impossibility. Anna is characteristically and exas-
peratingly impossible; and the English mind, practiced in all the
uses of indifference and compromise as the lubricants of daily life,
will never quite understand how she can be at once so keenly enlightened and so profoundly ingenuous. But Mrs. Wharton understands, and threads the whole glowing labyrinth of Anna's mind
without an instant of hesitation.

Anna would make a drama, joyful or deplorable as the case might
be, but certainly absorbing, out of any train of circumstances on
which she might turn her brooding attention. The lightest appeal
would rouse her courage and her loyalty, the simplest *cas de conscience* would call into play the whole armory of her doubts. Mrs.
Wharton has boldly produced a case which is far indeed from strain-
ing Anna's resources in the matter of double-edged spiritual scruples.
There is plenty to agonize her in the difficult question which she
has to answer in *The Reef*. The question there is what becomes of
her relation to Darrow, the relation which has finally asserted itself

as the most substantial fact in her dream-beset life, when she finds
she must adapt it to a view of him in which he seems unrecogniza-
ble. Her feeling for him does not change; the trouble would be less
if only it would. But that is not the way of emotion, which, as Anna
has to learn, will never show the least inclination to save us trouble.
It will not obey established facts, or lose its brightness on the mere
proof that the spring which fed it has been deflected. Darrow remains fully himself at the same time that, in the light of his hapless
adventure with Sophy, he appears other and strange; and Anna finds
on her hands two separate strains of impulse in regard to him which
must somehow be fused into one. Perhaps it is impossible; perhaps
she can just manage it. What is certain is that Sophy's more lucid
simplicity, her clearer eye for decisive action, put to shame the
luxuriance of Anna's hesitations. Sophy can act swiftly and self-
forgetfully, where Anna can only torture herself with questions
which after all refer to nothing but the saving or the losing of her
own happiness.

If in *The Custom of the Country* the spacious brilliance of the
scene is too much for Undine's tenuity, something of the sort, trans-
posed and reversed, has surely happened in *The Reef*. The difficulties which Anna is called on to deal with are handed over to
her in a form hardly worthy of her genius, and with a certain
abruptness which betrays Mrs. Wharton's tendency to reap her
harvest before it is ripe. It was in this case of the first importance
that the opening scenes should establish, beyond possibility of question, the inherence of Darrow's passage with Sophy in the texture
of the whole history. We must not only, that is to say, see Darrow
and Sophy thrown together at the start and be convinced of the steps
by which they became involved in their adventure, but we must be
quite certain, when we pick up their fortunes again later on, under
Anna's warm gaze, that they really are the same Darrow and the
same Sophy that we saw before. The fact is that on this point we
are not entirely reassured. Darrow himself is in any case a somewhat
pale figure, the least animated of the company; and if the marks
which he bears of the past are too slight, it may be because Mrs.
Wharton has scarcely succeeded in giving him substance enough
to show them. But with Sophy it is different. Sophy, romantically
established and occupied under Anna's roof, in the pale serenity

of the French autumn, is too graceful a figure in her tremulous
bravery for us to be doubtful about her. She is not the boyish young
adventuress, wind-ruffled and rain-brightened, whom we met on
Dover pier in the first chapter. This does not, of course, mean that
she might not have been—that she would never have done what
she is described as doing, or that, if she had, the young adventuress
would not have been softly transmuted by the silvery light of Givré.
But Sophy at Givré does not strike us as having undergone any
transmutation—she is merely a new acquaintance; and it is only
by an arbitrary act of authority on the part of the writer that the
events of the prologue become the discoveries which Anna has
presently to find a place for in her mind.

The prologue, with the use to which it is put, has, in short, to be
conceded to the author of *The Reef,* without too close enquiry as to
whether she has earned it; and perhaps after all it is conceded with
no great effort. For as soon as the shift is effected, and Anna has
taken her place as the center of vision, the action is all absorbed into
a certain mood and borne forward with a particular momentum in
which the difficulties of the transition are soon forgotten. The mood
is expressed in the romantic beauty of the old house, its worn and
wan and experienced distinction, not mellowed and enriched by its
long past (as an old English house would be) so much as patient
under the weight of it and still capable of anxious thought. Anna
brings to Givré her own simpler generosity of charm; and the youth
around her, the youth of her engaging young stepson and her de-
licious little daughter, the new sensitive youth of poor Sophy, steeps
the drama in the freshest of atmospheres and gives the impulse of
poetry to its movement. These chapters are undoubtedly the finest
that Mrs. Wharton has yet written. With the scene so prepared, the
air so alert with the intelligence of life, the presence of apprehended
pain and disaster must instantly be felt. Words are hardly needed;
knowledge comes with chance glimpses, a turn of the head, a
negligent movement, the slightest possible deflections from the
natural and the expected. Doubts and fears emerge, and the whole
train of consciousness, lapsing in a new direction, gathers pace and
becomes distress and bewilderment, without the necessity for one
violent stroke or emphasized effect. Here, then, is yet another and

a new attainment of Mrs. Wharton's fiction. She so rounds and fuses her subject, she throws over it the light of so receptive and intent a mood, that when once the development is started it carries itself through to the end, moving as one mass and needing no further impulsion.

The part played, in maintaining this equable flow, by Mrs. Wharton's use of striking and picturesque imagery, is too remarkable to be passed over. Imagery is commonly regarded as a kind of applied ornament, giving variety and relief to plain narrative; but it has a better justification than this when it is used as a structural part of the narrative itself. Mrs. Wharton has the rare gift of thinking naturally in images; they are not to her an added grace, but an immediate dramatization of a simple statement; and since a line of drama will always carry more weight than many lines of mere description, a pictorial symbol, so employed, economizes time and effort, supports and advances the narrative as well as adorns it. *The Reef* would give very many examples of this treatment of imagery, its impressment into the service of storytelling; though of course its practical help in any particular case cannot be measured without the full context. An isolated quotation only illustrates the vivid aptness of the picture, but it is worth illustrating:

> After that she no longer tried to laugh or argue her husband out of his convictions. They *were* convictions, and therefore unassailable. Nor was any insincerity implied in the fact that they sometimes seemed to coincide with hers. There were occasions when he really did look at things as she did; but for reasons so different as to make the difference between them all the greater. Life, to Mr. Leath, was like a walk through a carefully classified museum, where, in moments of doubt, one had only to look at the number and refer to one's catalogue; to his wife it was like groping about in a huge dark lumber-room, where the exploring ray of curiosity lit up now some shape of breathing beauty and now a mummy's grin.

In the English-speaking world there are always plenty of voices ready to explain to a deliberately trained and practiced artist like Mrs. Wharton the certain risks and likely failures of her method of work. Such a writer will be well-accustomed to hear that imagination is chilled by excessive attention to finish and design, that many of the greatest novelists have been careless of technical niceties, and that imperfect life is, at any rate, better than dead perfection. These assertions, undeniable and undenied, are not in themselves a great contribution to criticism, but they do, of course, point to a general truth of more interest. A writer ideally needs both a certain detachment from his material, so that he may grasp it as a whole, and also complete immersion in it, so that he may be aware of it with every nerve, never consciously using his powers of divination and deduction. Without the ability to stand over and away from his structure he can neither knit it firmly nor expose it squarely; but he cannot give it expressive value, the flush of life which is its very reason for existence, unless he has the affinity of long habit with the stuff he is working in. Of these two sides of the novelist's task it is obviously the first on which Mrs. Wharton is most at home; her books are the books of an imagination far more easily stimulated to work than induced to ruminate. Their curious lack of anything that could be disengaged as a philosophy of life, a characteristic synthesis of belief, is no doubt their weakness from one point of view, just as their fine clearcut outline is their strength from another. The mind that has never, so to say, compromised itself with life, that has kept its critical integrity entirely out of the way of imaginable superstition, must naturally pay for its fastidiousness in some sort; and it may well pay by the loss of the fullest possible intimacy with the stuff of character—especially of social character as opposed to individual—an intimacy more lightly won by the uncritical mind which does not know how to use it. There is accordingly a certain amount of Mrs. Wharton's work which shows the general defect of the *tour de force*—a defect, not of sinew or bone, but of vein and marrow. Such are the penalties of a talent whose leading qualities are swiftness and acuteness. But it is precisely in the case of a talent like this that summary inferences are most misleading, for its future can never be predicted. As time goes on its power is revealed by the fact that it begins to add to itself, right and left, the very virtues which appeared furthest from its reach, and to produce work which has gained in every respect, in freshness and vigor as in controlled flexibility, over its earlier experiments. This has been the history of the work of Mrs. Wharton; and, because it has not only had a history but is constantly making one, always attacking new positions and never repeating either a failure or a success, it is work of the kind most of all interesting to criticism, work of which, in the middle of its course, nothing can be foretold but that its best is yet to come.

Edith Wharton

by E. K. Brown

Edith Wharton never wished to be in the public eye. She lived for her art and her friends. The last years of her life were lonely for most of the men and the women she cared for were dead, and among younger people she did not find it easy to be intimate. The later chapters of her recollections, *A Backward Glance,* read almost like a series of obituaries for Henry James, for Howard Sturgis, the author of that forgotten novel *Belchamber,* for the two young war victims, Robert d'Humières and Ronald Simmons, for Minnie Bourget, the wife of the novelist, and for Walter Berry, who was the dearest of all. Since the recollections appeared three years ago, two other friends—among the oldest—have died: Paul Bourget and Bernard Berenson. To read her recollections is to feel that Edith Wharton's personal world collapsed in 1914 and has lain in ruins for more than a decade. She was a survivor, but she lived among the dead.

For thirty years she had resided almost continuously abroad. Her expatriation was not of her own doing. Her husband was obliged for the sake of his health to seek a climate not to be found in America, or, at least, in any part of America where he would have wished to live; and his wife accompanied him to Europe. She left America on the morrow, almost, of her first triumphant demonstration that she could make use of the world in which she moved for the purposes of tragic and ironic fiction. She had written *The House of Mirth,* with which, as she says, she "was turned from a drifting amateur into a professional," and she must now uproot herself

"Edith Wharton" by E. K. Brown. From *Études Anglaises,* 1938. Reprinted by permission of Mrs. E. K. Brown.

from the one little world that she really knew, from the little garden in which Henry James had said that she ought to be tethered.

She would have preferred England to France, but Edward Wharton would not consent to residence in England. The Whartons took a large apartment in Paris, in a quarter of embassies and palaces within view of the Invalides. As a reader of *The Age of Innocence* walks past that massive grandiose gray building in the rue de Varenne where Edith Wharton was to live for a decade, his mind turns to that passage where Newland Archer is approaching the apartment in which his cousin Ellen Olenska lives in her later years. He had known that she lived in the quarter of the Invalides; but he had thought of it as a rather dull mournful part of Paris, forgetting that it received radiance and even glory from the great golden dome. There were other sources of radiance and glory for the Whartons' apartment. From its front windows there must have been a great vista over the Seine and the expanse of ordered beauty from the Louvre to the Arc de Triomphe de l'Étoile. After the war Edith Wharton lived away from Paris, passing the winters in her medieval chateau at Hyères on the Riviera and the summers in the Pavillon Colombe, a beautiful low-lying eighteenth century house in the village of Saint-Brice-sous-forêt, a few miles beyond the suburbs of Paris. In both her homes she surrounded herself with books and flowers; it is doubtful which were the source of the sweeter pleasures.

No novelist has painted with a more severe truthfulness the emptiness which threatens the lives of those who live away from their own country. In *Madame de Treymes*, written just at the time when the Whartons took up residence in Paris, she had in the caricatured figures of Mr. and Mrs. Elmer Boykin given her judgment on the type of American for whom living in Europe is a profession. She tells us that the Boykins had left America because America was not adequate to the Boykin standard of luxury and distinction; they had left it not to fuse themselves in the life of France, but to take up an attitude of persistent niggling criticism towards that country, which bitterly offended them by carrying on its own mode of life just as if the Boykins had never crossed the Atlantic. No type of character is more frequently met in Edith

Wharton's fiction than the American expatriate whose life is a great void.

Her own life in France was no void. Her novels won for her admission into circles in which she moved happily and with a sense of being quietly at home. She had friends also in the larger or at least brisker world of politics and diplomacy. So fast was the pace of life in the rue de Varenne that it exhausted that prince of diners-out, Henry James, who alluded to it as a saraband and sought to resist its attraction. With the outbreak of war came an opportunity for her to feel even more intimately a part of France. The painter John Campton, whose delineation raises the novel *A Son at the Front* above mediocrity, debates the obligations to France of those who are not French but have found in France an environment in which they can live more happily and more effectively than in their own land. In his view such people owe more to France than the French themselves. That was also Edith Wharton's view. She acted on that view during the four years of war. She was tireless in charity and in hard dull work for the refugees from the devastated areas; the hours when she was not at work in hospitals or in committee-rooms she spent in writing about the war. There were few articles written to inform America about the course of events in France so vivid and at times so moving as those which were later collected in the book *Fighting France, from Dunkerque to Belfort*. So tireless was she that when she once allowed herself two or three months of absence from Paris she employed them in visiting Morocco and in preparing that tribute to Lyautey's miracle of colonization, *In Morocco*. Well might Henry James write of her nerves and muscles of steel! France was grateful; and since the war Edith Wharton might well feel that when she was living in France she was living at home.

As the years passed there was no doubt that she felt alienated from America. It was not that she abandoned America, but that her America was ceasing to exist; "to follow up its traces," as she says, "one had to come to Europe." Washington Irving speaks of the Hudson a century ago as bordered at one point by the "stately towers of the Joneses, the Schermerhornes and the Rhinelanders." It was from those towers that her ancestors came: her father was a Jones, her mother a Rhinelander, one of her grandparents a Schermerhorne. Their New York was that which Edith Wharton evokes in *The Age of Innocence, Old New York*, and in those delicately sure passages in *The Custom of the Country* which describe the background of Ralph Marvell. The plot of *The Custom of the Country* is indeed a symbol of the rejection, the humiliation of Edith Wharton's New York by the invaders from Pittsburgh, Chicago and points west. New York ceased to be a place where an old New Yorker of Mrs. Wharton's kind, a descendant of . . . Dutch gentry, could feel at home. The more New York changed the more nostalgic Edith Wharton became for that New York which was dead and which could never live again. Even its defects —its fear of ideas, its fear of strong emotions, its insular pride— seemed precious when set in contrast with the new chaos, the new clang of a civilization which had no center and did not even know what a civilization with a center meant.

Readers of her most recent novels, *Hudson River Bracketed* and *The Gods Arrive*, will have noted that at the center of them is a marriage between a girl who embodies the culture and the gentle civilization of old New York and a man who is an incarnation of the rough creative power of the West. The man is drawn to the girl because his imagination is haunted by the old code of conduct, the old way of life of New York, that attempt to form a new society which without being a copy of Europe would nevertheless preserve the essential values of life on the old continent. The girl is attracted to the man because of the power she divines in him, a power which contrasts with the charming impotence of the society in which she has grown up, a society which can enjoy with discrimination but has lost the power to create. The marriage was a stormy one; but Edith Wharton, who was clearly aware of the limited horizons, the timidity, the stuffiness of old New York, was bent on suggesting that whatever difficulties might lie in the way of the marriage, only when the energies of the West and the traditions of the old East are brought together can an adequate American civilization develop.

Although she liked to embody the fundamental conflicts of her novels in characters who represent differing social and geographical strata, her chief interest was not in the oppositions between the old New York and the new, between East and West, between aristocracy

→

and plutocracy, between America and Europe. It was an interest in values much more general and permanent. Many of these were aesthetic, some were social, some, in the old-fashioned Jamesian way, were moral. She believed in the gospel which in *The Ambassadors* Strether preaches to Little Bilham in Gloriani's garden: the welcoming of intense experience and the expression of one's deepest desires. She was a satiric and at times an angry critic of the puritanical morality and the conventionalism of the New York in which she lived as a girl. Her hostility to the puritanical and the conventional was much more serious than her impatience with the elements of chaos and incoherence in contemporary society. *Twilight Sleep* expresses a real resentment with the brash and giddy life of New York society in the Twenties; but the outcome of that novel, if painful, is not so hopelessly destructive to fine souls as the outcome of *The House of Mirth*, in which Lily Bart is the victim of a conventionalized society which is remorseless to those who deviate from its fixed ways. It would, of course, be fantastic to represent Edith Wharton as satisfied with a conception of life which bade one seek intense experience and ask no questions. She believed in taste; and she thought that the present day and the American continent in particular were sadly lacking in it. She believed indeed that without taste no satisfactory human society was possible. It is an old-fashioned belief; so is her conception of morality which is allied with it. Her morality, it is clear, is remote both from puritanical and conventional codes, which are in her view deadly enemies of true morality. Her morality is not easily defined; if I were pressed to set it down briefly I should say that it was the unwritten morality of the upper classes of Europe taken at its highest. It is not religious; few writers in Anglo-Saxon countries have been so indifferent to religion. It is not humanitarian; seldom has the problem of industrial justice appeared in her fiction, and in the one novel in which she did seek to present it fully, *The Fruit of the Tree*, her distance from realities merited the harsh comments that novel received from writers of the Left. It is not however purely individualistic; it is conscious of the individual's obligations to society at large. Divorce has always been bitterly opposed in her fiction: it appeared to her to be an unwarrantable sacrifice of the group to the individual, something which she detested as much as an unwarrantable sacrifice of the individual to the group. If asked to arbitrate in a given case between the good of the individual and the good of the group she would have fallen back on that nebulous criterion of taste and decided firmly as it dictated. Once she was a little more precise. In *The Mother's Recompense* Kate Clephane is confronted with a moral problem which is to her a bitter trial: shall she allow her daughter to marry a former lover of her own when she could prevent it by telling the girl the squalid story of her past? She takes that problem to the one clergyman in Edith Wharton's fiction who has any moral distinction. The criterion by which he decides is impressive: it represents one of Edith Wharton's deepest convictions about life. He says that he has a horror of "sterile pain." Accepting his advice Kate keeps her secret to herself and exiles herself from her daughter.

Somehow Edith Wharton both in her life and in her work seemed to have missed happiness. Something tense and thin and a little sharp marked both. Even in her poetry there is a lack of fullness, warmth and freedom. In a novel of which I cannot recall the title there is a bright phrase which strikingly differentiates her attitude to life from that of her great master. A young man is presented as leaving for Europe "uncled by Henry James and aunted, rather severely, by Edith Wharton." Beneath all the tensions of James, there was a place where life was sweet and warm; and despite the nervous precisions of his technique, despite the supersubtle distinctions on which he delighted to linger, there was something large and rich about his work which is absent from that of his most accomplished disciple.

Into Edith Wharton's life there would be an indelicacy in prying further. There was a tragedy in it which was veiled proudly even from many who knew her well. Unless she herself may have chosen that after her death the veil be removed, it should not be lifted. It is to her work that she would wish attention to be devoted; to her life and character only in so far as knowledge of them proved indispensable to illuminate her work.

Conscious art was the basis of all she wrote. When somewhat late in her development she began to associate intimately with other writers she was astonished and distressed to find that "few of them were greatly interested in the deeper processes of the art; their con-

scious investigations seldom go deeper than syntax." They seemed
to be in quest of attractive and rewarding subjects; she, crushed
by the multitude of subjects calling for presentation, was in quest
of the exactly right mode of presenting a subject, the mode which
would bring out every last iota of possibility the subject had. *Ethan
Frome* is perhaps the most moving of her subjects; yet, in her preface—written, it is true, many years after the book—her whole interest is in explaining and vindicating the form she chose. The
problem with which she wrestled was not the nature of Ethan
Frome himself, or of his shy love for his wife's cousin, or of his
utter frustration as engineer, farmer and person; it was a technical
problem: it lay in the fact that the subject was one "of which the
dramatic climax, or rather the anticlimax, occurs a generation later
than the first acts of the tragedy," such an "enforced lapse of time"
suggesting that the appropriate form would be the full-length novel,
while Edith Wharton was sure on other grounds that the appropriate form was the nouvelle. She felt that the stark and inarticulate
natures of the characters would be betrayed in a full-length novel.
She feared that the incompatibility between the exigencies of the
characterization and the exigencies of the time-element in the situation might make the subject an unmanageable one, might indicate
that it was a siren subject which she ought to reject. She decided
that it was not a siren subject but simply a difficult one; and she
devised an extremely complicated mode of presentation by which
it might be compressed within the bounds of the nouvelle. Her
concern in the preface is all with matters of art; and had she written
prefaces for all her works of fiction (and that she did not is a profound pity, for she was singularly acute in what she said of her
own works) there is no doubt that in them she would have raised
problems of dimension, perspective, true and false use of dialogue
and monologue, the focal character.

   In her early works, those nouvelles and collections of short stories
which seem so slight and brittle when reread today, she used a
style which was brilliantly emphatic and almost provocatively artificial. In books such as *The Greater Inclination* and *Crucial
Instances* there is a crackle of epigram and near-epigram which
distracts the reader from the states of mind of the characters and
even from the progress of the story, and at times suggests that the

matter of the work was found valuable only as a succession of pegs for dazzling comments. Later Edith Wharton came to prefer a style more supple and quiet. Her writing was at its best in the seven or eight years before the war, in books such as *The Reef* (where the mark of James's later manner is a little obtrusive, however), *The Hermit and the Wild Woman, Ethan Frome* and *The Custom of the Country.* In these books she avoids the over-tenseness which had been the vice of the early period and the over-softness which was later to reduce her writing to the merest commonplace in long stretches of the last novels and nouvelles.

Indeed it was in those years just before the war that her art in all its aspects was at its best. It was at that time she wrote her bitter and powerful novel of manners, *The Custom of the Country.* For the novel of manners her gifts were not at first sight impressive. Her direct knowledge of America was slight; and she had no opportunities for enlarging it. She knew New York, and as the moving nouvelle *The Bunner Sisters* showed, her New York was not simply that of the aristocrats and the plutocrats; she knew the back country of New England as she had shown in *Ethan Frome,* and was about to show in *Summer;* but even if one adds Newport, as *The Age of Innocence* allows one to do, her knowledge is still confined within a narrow area. She was a tireless traveler; but her travels took her across the Atlantic, not across the Alleghanies. The reader of her novels will feel that to her Chicago was much more alien than Crete; and he will be right. Nor was her point of view, her essential and natural point of view, a fruitful one from which to survey the American scene. She was an aristocrat and an artist; she grew up among people who did not interest themselves in politics, which in New York had got into quite other hands, and who detested the new methods of business in their city—methods which they thought, not without reason, irreconcilable with decent standards of public morality. The business of New York was in the grip of the invaders. About those invaders she knew a great deal; and, wisely, in her novel of manners she sought to represent American life as a conflict between certain old loyalties represented by her New York and certain new drives which she embodied in the people who had come from all the minor centers of business in the country to lay siege to New York. Instead of dealing with the Spragg family—

who represent the invasion—as they had been in their earlier days in Apex City, she sought to show what they became in New York. Wise too was her decision to represent the family chiefly through its women, making Mr. Spragg a somewhat drab background. She overcame the huge deficiencies of her knowledge remarkably well. If one allows her the choice of a predominantly feminine point of view, the novel cannot but seem illuminating and profound. It shows an ability to grapple with the meaning of large ethical and social movements (as *The Valley of Decision* had shown, in the panorama of tendencies in eighteenth century Italy) and an ability to make important deductions as to the drift of American life.

It was in the prewar years also that she accomplished her most penetrating exploration of character. *The Reef* is the deepest of her soundings of human nature; and had she not written it no one could have supposed that she had the power to see so clearly and with such compassion what the tragic complications of experience can mean. In George Darrow, as Mr. Robert Morss Lovett has said, she has made her answer to the critics who have scoffed at her handling of male character: Darrow is the most revealing study she has presented of the cultivated sensitive uncertain man of leisure who is always emerging in her books and who offers a difficult but rewarding opportunity for the novelist who delights in subtle portraiture. In Anna Summers Leath, Edith Wharton sets before us the type of the entirely civilized American woman (the fictional equivalent of herself): a woman whose emotions are held in severe check by her training and her associations, but who, half unknown to herself, places the ideal in a human relationship—a great love— in which she can find absolute release and serenity and a sense of escape from the bonds of civilization which are gently strangling her. Henry James was deeply moved by the book. Hyperbole came easily to his generous nature when he sought to define the quality of anything that a friend had done; and doubtless he took too intense a tone when he spoke of the book's "supreme validity and distinction," of "the unspeakably *fouillée* nature of the situation between the two principals," and of Anna as an "exquisite thing, and with her characteristic, finest scarce differentiated notes . . . sounded with a wonder of delicacy." The sharpness and thinness characteristic of Edith Wharton are however absent from this novel, at least from all but the opening pages which strike, not too happily, the note of satire and irony. The warmth and fullness which Edith Wharton seemed to lack more than most novelists of her time suffuse the description of Anna's states of feeling and bathe the chateau of Givré, where the tragic complications work themselves out, in a mellow and silvered light which is strangely like that which fills the marvellous first chapter of *The Portrait of a Lady*. Anna Leath and George Darrow belong to Edith Wharton's own little world, the tight little world of old New York families. So do most of her living characters: Selden and Lily Bart in *The House of Mirth*, Ralph Marvell in *The Custom of the Country*, old Mr. Longhope and his confidante Mrs. Ansell in *The Fruit of the Tree*; Ellen Archer Olenska and her cousin Newland in *The Age of Innocence*; Halo Spear in *Hudson River Bracketed* and *The Gods Arrive*. These are her successes; but they are not rounded vital people like the characters in fiction that Edith Wharton most admired—the people who make *War and Peace* almost conterminous with life itself. Her creative power was not that of the masters of fiction: she caught aspects of people rather than their central principle, their oddities, their saliencies, not their fundamental humanity. Even with Ethan Frome, his wife and her cousin there is something amiss: the characterization seems subordinate to the situation and the treatment. The impression left by that artistic achievement is that of strange, pathetic, twisted figures almost of another species from that of the author and her mouthpiece, the engineer.

It can not be chiefly for characterization that Edith Wharton will continue to be read. It will be because of her interest in technique, an interest which makes her novels and her shorter pieces of fiction suggestive to the reader who cares, as she did, about the processes of art. It will also be because of the clarity of her social observation: she happened to know certain corners of American life extraordinarily well, and it has happened that these corners have had no other comparable historian. Finally it will be because of the temper of her mind, which has given a special tone to her best writing, not the tone of the highest art indeed, but a tone which is unfailingly interesting and stimulating, that "particular fine asperity" which Henry James spoke of in summing up her intelligence.

In her work there is a vast amount which is ephemeral. Her first book of fiction was not published until she was thirty-four. She is dead at seventy-five. Within forty years she brought out ten collections of tales, ten nouvelles in book form, and thirteen novels; to this must be added two volumes of verse, books about gardens and houses, books about travel in France, Italy and Morocco, a study of French life and a study of the art of fiction, a volume of reminiscences, two translations from the German and prefaces to the works of friends. It is a vast performance, and little of it will endure.

It is doubtless a piece of folly to attempt at this time to distinguish in her work between the ephemeral and the enduring. But it is a kind of folly at once attractive and useful. What will certainly endure, is I think, readily stated: a great technical experiment, *Ethan Frome*; a distinguished novel of manners, *The Custom of the Country*, a distinguished novel of situation, *The Mother's Recompense*, and a distinguished novel of character and tone, *The Reef*; some evocations of old New York, notably *The Age of Innocence*, and some nouvelles in the series *Old New York*; a dozen stories of the macabre and the supernatural; and finally the explorations of her art, of which some have been collected in *The Writing of Fiction*, and others are to be found in the files of the great American reviews.

Henry James's Heiress:
The Importance of Edith Wharton

by Q. D. Leavis

The unfinished posthumous novel of Edith Wharton just published [1] should at least serve to bring up this author's name for
evaluation. It is incidentally quite worth reading if you are an
amateur of the period now in fashion again (the Seventies). It
would have been far more worth publishing if Mrs. Wharton's
literary executor had supplemented his appendix by a memoir and
critical essay designed to introduce the present generation to her
best work, scarcely ever read in England—for, to the educated
English public, Mrs. Wharton's novels are those of her last ten
years and known vaguely as the kind of fiction which was published
serially in *Good Housekeeping*. But her characteristic work was all
done long before, early enough for one of her good novels to have
been published in World's Classics in 1936, more than thirty years
after it was first printed. It was as the historian of New York society
of the Nineties that she first achieved character and eminence as a
novelist, on the dual grounds, as she said, that it was "a field as
yet unexploited by any novelist who had grown up in that little
hot-house of traditions and conventions" and had been "tacitly regarded as unassailable." In her rapid growth as combined social
critic and historian, she continued to strike roots outwards and
downwards until she had included in her reach the lowest levels of
rustic, urban, and manufacturing life. And her work was no mere
historical fictionizing—she was a serious novelist. She was also an

[1] *The Buccaneers* (Appleton Century, 1938).

extraordinarily acute and far-sighted social critic; in this she was original and appears still more so when we think with what an effort this detachment must have been achieved by the child brought up to believe it her ambition to become, like her mother, the best-dressed woman in New York, and who was married young to an anti-intellectual society man.

By a combination of circumstances, she was peculiarly qualified to undertake such work. Her interesting autobiography documents her cultural origins for us. There we are told that the best people in New York, among whom she was born, had the traditions of a mercantile middle class whose "value lay in upholding two standards of importance in any community, that of education and good manners, and of scrupulous probity in business affairs." This society was leisured, and satisfied with a moderate wealth—she never in her young days encountered the gold-fever in any form. It concentrated on the arts of living that radiate from home-making. It was resolutely English in culture (speaking "pure English," importing tutors and governesses, reading the English classics and deploring contemporary American men of letters) and habitually traveled abroad (unlike Boston) though keeping aloof from the English court and society. She grew up to see this society disintegrate from within, its values succumbing to spiritual anemia—"the blind dread of innovation and the instinctive shrinking from responsibility" that she noted as its chief weaknesses and which left politics to be the prey of business—even before its standards were overthrown by the invasion from without of the predatory new rich. Her quick intelligence made her aware of the import of changes that even an insider at the time could only have sensed, her literary ambition encouraged her to try to fix them in the novel, and her early environment and family traditions gave her a position from which to survey changes in the social scene, a code by which to judge the accompanying shifts in mores and values by which to estimate the profit and loss. Her admiration of Henry James's work, later her great intimacy with him, provided her with a springboard from which to take off as an artist.

For her literary career began, as she said, "in the days when Thomas Hardy, in order to bring out *Jude the Obscure* in a leading New York periodical, was compelled to turn the children of Jude and Sue into adopted orphans; when the most popular magazine in America excluded all stories containing any reference to 'religion, love, politics, alcohol, or fairies' (this is textual); the days when a well known New York editor, offering me a large sum for the serial rights of a projected novel, stipulated only that no reference to 'an unlawful attachment' should figure in it . . . and when the translator of Dante, Professor Eliot Norton, hearing (after the appearance of *The House of Mirth*) that I was preparing another 'society' novel, wrote in alarm imploring me to remember that 'no great work of the imagination has ever been based on illicit passion'!" It was equivalent to the literary England of Trollope's beginnings, yet Edith Wharton without any bravado assumed that because she did not depend on literature for her income she should ignore its "incurable moral timidity" and the displeasure of her social group. "The novelist's best safeguard is to write only for that dispassionate and ironic critic who dwells within the breast," she wrote. The likeness to Jane Austen is revealed in that, and borne out by her decision, after writing several dull psychological novels, to make a novel out of what she knew best, the fashionable New York of her early married life "in all its flatness and futility." In doing so she was taking up Henry James's work where he left it off with *The Bostonians* and *The Portrait of a Lady*. And in this novel [*The House of Mirth*] she turned, as she noted, from an amateur into a professional novelist. The American novel grew up with Henry James and achieved a tradition with Mrs. Wharton. He, she points out in a passage of great interest,[2] was never at home in twentieth century America—"he belonged irrevocably to the old America out of which I also came" and whose last traces, as she said, remained in Europe whither he fortunately went to seek them. "Henry James was essentially a novelist of manners, and the manners he was qualified by nature and situation to observe were those of the little vanishing group of people among whom he had grown up, or their more picturesque prototypes in older societies—he often bewailed to me his total inability to use the 'material,' financial and industrial, of modern American life." And she instances James's failure to make plausible Mr. Verver in *The Golden Bowl* or "to relate either him or his native 'American City' to any sort

[2] *A Backward Glance*, pp. 175-76.

of concrete reality." She might have instanced her own Mr. Spragg and his Apex City in contrast, those fully realized symbols which make the later creations *Babbitt* and *Main Street* seem unnecessary as well as crude work. Unlike James, she rightly felt herself qualified to deal with the society that succeeded "the old America" and she stayed to write its natural history, to write it in a form as shapely and with a surface as finished as if she had had a number of predecessors in her chosen task. These works had the advantage of being "readable" as Jane Austen's and even George Eliot's were and as *The Ambassadors* was not. It is profitable to observe how, in *The Custom of the Country*, she makes use of James's technique and yet reaches a public unwilling or unable to wrestle with his formidable novels.

She was early convinced that the virtue had gone out of "the old America" of her ancestors: "When I was young it used to seem to me that the group in which I grew up was like an empty vessel into which no new wine would ever again be poured." So when she decided to make a novel out of the circle in which she lived she chose to depict it in terms of "the slow disintegration" of Lily Bart, one of the "wasted human possibilities" who form, she declared, "the underpinning [on which] such social groups (the shallow and the idle) always rest." No doubt it was her own experience that enabled her to isolate the destructive element in such societies—"the quality of making other standards nonexistent by ignoring them. . . . Lily's set had a force of negation which eliminated everything beyond their own range of perception." These explanations are from the subsequent introduction. In the novel (*The House of Mirth*, 1905) this analysis is present in solution—in terms of dialogue, dramatic situation, and the process by which the exquisite Lily Bart slips down into annihilation. For in these novels Mrs. Wharton never ceases to be first of all a novelist. Her social criticism is effected in the terms that produced Middlemarch society and the Dodsons in *The Mill on the Floss*, and often challenges comparison with analogous effects in Jane Austen:

> Mrs. Gryce had a kind of impersonal benevolence: cases of individual need she regarded with suspicion, but she subscribed to Institutions when their annual reports showed an impressive surplus.

In her youth, girls had not been supposed to require close supervision. They were generally assumed to be taken up with the legitimate
business of courtship and marriage, and interference in such affairs on
the part of their natural guardians was considered as unwarrantable
as a spectator's suddenly joining in a game. There had of course been
"fast" girls even in Mrs. Peniston's early experience; but their fastness,
at worst, was understood to be a mere excess of animal spirits, against
which there could be no graver charge than that of being "unladylike." The modern fastness appeared synonymous with immorality,
and the mere idea of immorality was as offensive to Mrs. Peniston as
a smell of cooking in the drawing-room: it was one of the conceptions
her mind refused to admit.

[Of the much-divorced but "ineradicably innocent" beauty from
the West.] The lady's offenses were always against taste rather than
conduct; her divorce record seemed due to geographical rather than
ethical conditions; and her worst laxities were likely to proceed from
a wandering and extravagant good nature.

The feature of most permanent interest in the book is the systematic
portrayal of the various groups in New York society. These are
created with zest and an abundant life, surprisingly lacking animus;
even distaste is lost in ironic appreciation. And no group or character is wantonly dragged in, each has an indispensable function in
advancing the plot. They range from the timid millionaire of the
old school, Percy Gryce:

After attaining his majority, and coming into the fortune which the
late Mr. Gryce had made out of a patent device for excluding fresh
air from hotels, the young man continued to live with his mother in
Albany; but on Jefferson Gryce's death, when another large property
passed into her son's hands, Mrs. Gryce thought that what she called
his "interests" demanded his presence in New York. She accordingly
installed herself in the Madison Avenue house, and Percy, whose
sense of duty was not inferior to his mother's, spent all his week-days
in the handsome Broad Street office, where a batch of pale men on
small salaries had grown gray in the management of the Gryce estate,
and where he was initiated with becoming reverence into every detail
of the art of accumulation. . . .

through the established "good" society—smart Trenors, dowdy van
Osburghs, and their parasites like the divorcée Mrs. Fisher—to the
various social aspirants, such as the new-rich Gormans:

Mrs. Fisher's unconventionality was, after all, a merely superficial divergence from an inherited social creed, while the manners of the Gorman circle represented their first attempt to formulate such a creed for themselves. . . .

the comic Wellington Brys and the financier Rosedale (not stock size) down to the outermost darkness of Mrs. Norma Hatch from the West, "rich, helpless, unplaced," living in the Emporium Hotel whence she endeavors to launch herself into the bosom of society. [There is an invaluable pre-Sinclair Lewis account of fashionable hotel life of the time]:

The environment in which Lily found herself was as strange to her as its inhabitants. She was unacquainted with the world of the fashionable New York hotel—a world over-heated, over-upholstered, and over-fitted with mechanical appliances for the gratification of fantastic requirements, while the comforts of a civilized life were as unattainable as in a desert. Through this atmosphere of torrid splendor moved wan beings as richly upholstered as the furniture, beings without definite pursuits or permanent relations. . . . Somewhere behind them, in the background of their lives, there was doubtless a real past, peopled by real human activities: they themselves were probably the product of strong ambitions, persistent energies, diversified contacts with the wholesome roughness of life; yet they had no more real existence than the poet's shades in limbo.

Lily had not been long in this pallid world without discovering that Mrs. Hatch was its most substantial figure. That lady, though still floating in the void, showed faint symptoms of developing an outline. . . . It was, in short, as the regulator of a germinating social life that Miss Bart's guidance was required; her ostensible duties as secretary being restricted by the fact that Mrs. Hatch, as yet, knew hardly any one to write to. . . . Compared with the vast gilded void of Mrs. Hatch's existence, the life of Lily's former friends seemed packed with ordered activities. Even the most irresponsible pretty woman of her acquaintance had her inherited obligations, her conventional benevolences, her share in the working of the great civic machine; and all hung together in the solidarity of these traditional functions. . . .

Mrs. Hatch swam in a haze of indeterminate enthusiasms, aspirations culled from the stage, the newspapers, the fashion journals, and a gaudy world of sport still more completely beyond her companion's ken. . . . The difficulty was to find any point of contact between her ideals and Lily's.

Such a combination of sustained anthropological interest with literary ability was hitherto unknown to fiction except in *The Bostonians*. Mrs. Wharton had all the qualifications that Galsworthy so disastrously lacked; to place *The Forsyte Saga* beside one of her characteristic novels is to expose it.

The Custom of the Country (1913) is undoubtedly her masterpiece. . . . Here the theme is explicitly "social disintegration." But now the "good" New York society has shrunk to a sideshow, the center is consciously occupied by the moneyed barbarians; they lack both a moral and a social code but are fast acquiring the latter by imitation. Whereas old New York (like Henry James's Boston) by keeping itself to itself had evolved an independent culture, new New York is shown trying to construct an imitation of European culture by copying its social surface, by acquiring it by marriage, by buying up its antiques, and by reproducing its architectural masterpieces at home:

> Bowen, from his corner, surveyed a seemingly endless perspective of plumed and jewelled heads, of shoulders bare or black-coated encircling the close-packed tables. During some forty years' perpetual exercise of his perceptions he had never come across anything that gave them the special titillation produced by the sight of the dinner hour at the Nouveau Luxe: the same sense of putting his hand on human nature's passion for the factitious, its incorrigible habit of imitating the imitation. As he sat watching the familiar faces swept towards him on the rising tide of arrival—for it was one of the joys of the scene that the type was always the same even when the individual was not—he hailed with renewed appreciation this costly expression of a social ideal. The dining room at the Nouveau Luxe represented, on such a spring evening, what unbounded material power had devised for the delusion of its leisure: a phantom "society," with all the rules, smirks, gestures of its model, but evoked out of promiscuity and incoherence while the other had been the product of continuity and choice. And the instinct which had driven a new class of world-compellers to bind themselves to slavish imitation of the superseded, and their prompt and reverent faith in the reality of the sham they had created, seemed to Bowen the most satisfying proof of human permanence.
>
> Small, cautious, middle-class, had been the ideals of aboriginal New York; but they were singularly coherent and respectable as contrasted with the chaos of indiscriminate appetites which made up its modern

tendencies. . . . What Popple called society was really just like the
houses it lived in: a muddle of misapplied ornament over a thin
steel shell of utility. The steel shell was built up in Wall Street, the
social trimmings were hastily added in Fifth Avenue; and the union
between them was as monstrous and factitious, as unlike the gradual
homogeneous growth which flowers into what other countries know
as society, as that between the Blois gargoyles on Peter van Degen's
roof and the skeleton walls supporting them.

The writing is unbrokenly taut and incisive, with sustained local
vitality. The hero reflects on his "aboriginal family"—"Harriet
Ray, sealed up tight in the vacuum of inherited opinion, where
not a breath of fresh sensation could get at her," "hardly anything
that mattered to him existed for them, and their prejudices reminded him of signposts warning off trespassers who have long
since ceased to intrude." Instead of the downward drift characteristic of *The House of Mirth*, we are initiated into the triumphant
social and material progress of Undine Spragg, type of the new
as Lily Bart was of the superseded. Thanks to an inborn lack
of either moral sense or introspective qualms, Undine hauls herself
to the top of the ladder—trampling husbands, family decencies, and
social codes underfoot, perpetually violating in all unconsciousness
even her own moral professions. Yet Undine is not a monster. She
is felt to be less of one than Rosamund Vincy, George Eliot's masterpiece on the same pattern, and there is a stimulus to be derived
from the display of her tactics. The pattern of this novel lends itself to a kind of irony congenial to Mrs. Wharton—the latent irony
that is to be discovered in certain kinds of situation: the clash
between civilized and primitive mores, between pretense and actuality, intention and achievement. Her novels are rich in social
comedy, displayed with something like Jane Austen's enjoyment,
though the victory does not, as in the latter's works, go to the finer
spirits.

The next novel in this line is *Twilight Sleep* (1927), which displays the chaos that followed on the establishment of a society based
on money without any kind of traditions. It is inferior to the earlier
work in its tendency to come down on the side of the farcical in
the study of Pauline Manford, whose optimistic progress through
life is symbolized in the title.

"Of course there ought to be no Pain . . . nothing but Beauty. . . . It ought to be one of the loveliest, most poetic things in the world to have a baby," Mrs. Manford declared, in that bright efficient voice which made loveliness and poetry sound like the attributes of an advanced industrialism, and babies something to be turned out in series like Fords.

Nevertheless it compares favorably with Huxley's and other novels treating of the same kind of life. Pauline, whose millions were made in the Middle West from the manufacture of motors, appears intended to embody the crude virtues of the invaders of pioneer stock, for with all her innocence of culture and her belief in activity for its own sake and her muddled passion for universal spiritual progress—in spite of this she is seen to have a respectable aspect too. For opposed to her is the next generation, represented by her daughter-in-law and her social group, whose insolent irresponsibility and empty vice set off whatever it was worth admiring—some moral positive or intuitive decency?—that at least kept the family from going to pieces, that Edith Wharton felt even a Pauline Manford retained but was then (in the Twenties) melting away under her eyes: the last stage of the social disintegration she had analyzed and chronicled and turned into art. She had lived, she felt, to see disappear "the formative value of nearly three hundred years of social observance: the concreted living up to long-established standards of honor and conduct, of education and manners."

This sequence leads up to the fiction of Scott Fitzgerald, Faulkner and Kay Boyle, among others, and without it their writings cannot be understood by the English reader. This school depicts (Faulkner and Kay Boyle with approval) a kind of life, without roots or responsibilities, where value is attributed only to drunkenness and allied states of excess. This phase of American culture is conveniently illustrated by the career of the late Harry Crosby. Mrs. Wharton's autobiography contains a first-hand account of the earlier half of this cultural disintegration. Read in sequence, after *The Education of Henry Adams* and Henry James's *A Small Boy and Others,* and before Malcolm Cowley's *Exile's Return*, it provides the English student with part of this indispensable background to American literature—the cultural history of literary America which, if Van

Wyck Brooks's *The Flowering of New England* had been executed
by an able critic, would now be complete to date in five volumes.

Later on she attempted to supplement her sequence by historical
studies—*The Age of Innocence* (1920) and *Old New York* (1924)—
of the static society of her grandparents' days. But the historical
novel necessarily bears about the same relation to art as the wax-
work, and in any case her talents found congenial only the contemporary and the changing. Here she has to reproduce "the old
New York way of taking life 'without effusion of blood.'"

Nevertheless there are good things in both books. One remembers
the analysis of

> . . . that terrifying product of the social system he belonged to and
> believed in, the young girl who knew nothing and expected every-
> thing. His own exclamation: "Women should be free—as free as we
> are," struck to the root of a problem that it was agreed in his world
> to regard as nonexistent. "Nice" women, however wronged, would
> never claim the kind of freedom he meant, and generous-minded men
> like himself were therefore—in the heat of argument—the more
> chivalrously ready to concede it them. Such verbal generosities were
> in fact only a humbugging disguise of the inexorable convention that
> tied things together and bound people down to the old pattern. In
> reality they all lived in a kind of hieroglyphic world, where the real
> thing was never said or done or even thought, but only represented by
> a set of arbitrary signs. . . . The result, of course, was that the young
> girl who was the center of this elaborate system of mystification re-
> mained the more inscrutable for her very frankness and assurance.
> She was frank, poor darling, because she had nothing to conceal,
> assured because she knew of nothing to be on her guard against. . . .
> But when he had gone the brief round of her he returned discouraged
> by the thought that all this frankness and innocence were only an
> artificial product. Untrained human nature was not frank and inno-
> cent; it was full of the twists and deferences of an instinctive guile.

After this sequence she ceased to write novels worthy of herself.
Partly she was growing old; partly, as she wrote in her memoirs,
she should have ceased to write because "the world she had grown
up in and been formed by had been destroyed in 1914."

But her work is by no means so limited as this may have suggested, even though suggestions have been made that she turned

Henry James's early work from a sport to the beginning of a tradition, that she was the nearest thing to an American Jane Austen, and the archetype of a Galsworthy. As far back as 1907 she had shown, in *The Fruit of the Tree,* her recognition of the general social problem and her refusal to limit her subject-matter to the moneyed or educated strata of Americans. Heaven knows where she got her knowledge of mill-towns, but here, though the novel is uncertain in intention and now only readable in patches, she revealed the split between the capitalist ruling class and the oppressed mill-hands, the worthlessness of the lives of the one and the misery of the lives of the other. Nor do we know how she acquired the material for that moving study of the sufferings of the respectable poor, the story *The Bunner Sisters.* Mrs. Wharton's presentation of the poor (of New York in the horse-car period in this story, of the hill-farm folk in *Ethan Frome* [1911], and of the New England rustics in *Summer* [1917]) is like George Eliot's in its sympathy and its freedom from sentimental evasions, but without the latter's large nobility that throws a softening light on all wretchedness. She is prone to end on a note of suspension in fierce irony that was not included in George Eliot's make-up. Mrs. Wharton, with her unmannered style and impersonal presentation, solved the problem of tone by ignoring the reader altogether. These three nouvelles might well be issued in England in one volume; everyone interested in literature ought to read them at least once—they are works of art, and historically they have some importance. She was the first to outrage the accepted pretense of seeing the New England countryside idyllically. Hers was informed realism.

> For years I had wanted to draw life as it really was in the derelict mountain villages of New England, a life even in my time, and a thousandfold more a generation earlier, utterly unlike that seen through the rose-colored spectacles of my predecessors, Mary Wilkins and Sarah Orne Jewett. In those days the snowbound villages of western Massachusetts were still grim places, morally and physically; insanity, incest, and slow mental and moral starvation were hidden away behind the paintless wooden housefronts. *Ethan Frome* was written after I had spent ten years in the hill region where the scene is laid, during which years I had come to know well the aspect, dialect, and mental and moral attitude of the hill people.

In consequence *Summer*, and the inferior but better-known *Ethan Frome*, stand, along with the Scottish specimen, *The House with the Green Shutters*, in the *Wuthering Heights* category.

Mrs. Wharton's interest in the contemporary social scene then was deep and wide as well as acute and witty. *Silas Marner* is rightly considered a classic of our language, but except for the accidental advantage of having a more attractive social picture to reproduce—a mellower setting, less ungracious mores, a more comely dialect—it seems to me inferior to *Summer*. The village of North Dormer, "abandoned of men, left apart by all the forces that link life to life in modern communities," where only those remain who can't get away or who have drifted back wrecked, completes Mrs. Wharton's social survey. Outside North Dormer is the Mountain, the home of a colony of squatters, bad characters and outlaws, who represent the limits of degradation to which society can sink—they have neither material civilization nor moral tradition. Mrs. Wharton declared that they were drawn in every detail from life. She was bold enough to seize on the Mountain for an unforgettable symbol that few novelists would have cared or dared to touch (it was received, she recorded, "with indignant denial by reviewers and readers"). And the understanding shown in these three stories of the workings of uneducated, rustic, and similar inarticulate kinds of minds is more convincing than George Eliot's, even as hers is more plausible than Hardy's, both these last having a suspicious tendency to humorous effects and George Eliot besides being never quite free from a shade of superiority in her attitude to intellectual inferiors.

Edith Wharton's value seems to me therefore not merely, as Mr. Edmund Wilson said in a recent article ("Justice to Edith Wharton," *The New Republic*, June 29th, 1938) that she wrote "in a period (1905-1917) when there were few American writers worth reading." I am convinced that anyone interested in the cultural basis of society, and anyone sensitive to quality in the novel, will find this selection of her writings I have made of permanent worth and unique in character. The final question then is, what order of novelist is she?—*i.e.*, not how permanent but how good? She was, until her decay, a tough-minded, robust artist, not the shrinking minor writer or the ladylike talent. It is characteristic that she should refer to "that dispassionate and ironic critic who dwells within the breast" of authors, and equally so that she should have considered the unencouraging atmosphere (indifference to her literary success and disapproval of her choosing to write) of her family and social circle, and the adverse reviews she received from outside, stimulating to talent, just as she accepted the severest professional criticism as valuable. This, she said, was better for fostering literary ability than "premature flattery and local celebrity" and having one's path smoothed; one contrasts this with Mrs. Woolf's claims for the creative temperament. She was a born artist; of the work of her prime she could justly say "My last page is latent in my first." Of how many novels in the English language before hers can that be said? She had the advantage of being a solidly-educated lady frequenting the most cultivated society of England and France. As an artist she had Henry James behind her work, whereas Sinclair Lewis, when he later attempted similarly to epitomize his environment in fiction, had only H. G. Wells behind his. She was remarkably intelligent; it is easy as well as more popular to be wise after the event (like Sinclair Lewis) but it takes a kind of genius to see your culture from the outside, to diagnose what is happening and plot its curves contemporaneously as she did. Jane Austen never got outside (of course she could never have imagined doing so): her social criticism is all from the inside and remains indoors without so much as a glance out of the window. It is not only that in Jane Austen social forces never come up for comment or that she accepts the theory of the rich man in his castle and the poor man at his gate, but that she can mention the enclosure of the commons as the natural subject of conversation for the gentlemen at dinner—just that and no more. Yet there can be no question that Jane Austen was a great novelist while Edith Wharton's greatest admirer would not claim that title for her. What makes a great novelist? Apparently not intelligence or scope or a highly-developed technique, though, other things being equal, they often give an advantage. But what then are the other things?

Again, compare Edith Wharton with George Eliot. George Eliot was a simple-minded woman except where great sensitiveness of feeling gave her a subtle insight—even her learning was deployed with solemn simplicity. Undeniably Mrs. Wharton had a more flexible mind, she was both socially and morally more experienced than George Eliot and therefore better able to enter into uncongenial states of feeling and to depict as an artist instead of a preacher distasteful kinds of behavior. Her Undine Spragg is better sustained and handled than the other's Rosamund Vincy. Undine's sphere of action is dazzling and she always has a fresh surprise for us up her sleeve in the way of moral obtuseness; it was cleverer to make Undine end up at the top of the tree with her only disappointment that her last husband couldn't get made Ambassador (on account of having a divorced wife) than to involve herself in disasters like Rosamund: the manifold irony of worldly success is more profitable than any simple moral lesson and artistically how much richer! Mrs. Wharton writes better than George Eliot, who besides lacking grace rarely achieves the economy of language that Mrs. Wharton commands habitually. Her technique is absolutely right and from the works I have instanced it would be difficult to alter or omit without harm, for, like Henry James, she was the type of conscious artist writing to satisfy only her own inflexible literary conscience. Now George Eliot in general moves like a cart-horse and too often takes the longest way round. But again it is George Eliot who is the great novelist.

I think it eventually becomes a question of what the novelist has to offer us, either directly or by implication, in the way of positives. In *The Bunner Sisters, Summer,* and some other places, Mrs. Wharton rests upon the simple goodness of the decent poor, as indeed George Eliot and Wordsworth both do in part—that is, the most widespread common factor of moral worth. But beyond that Mrs. Wharton has only negatives, her values emerging I suppose as something other than what she exposes as worthless. This is not very nourishing, and it is on similar grounds that Flaubert, so long admired as the ideal artist of the novel, has begun to lose esteem. It seems to be the fault of the disintegrating and spiritually impoverished society she analyzes. Her value is that she does analyze and is not content to reflect. We may contrast Jane Austen, who does not even analyze, but, having the good fortune to have been born into a flourishing culture, can take for granted its foundations and accept its standards, working within them on a basis of internal relations entirely. The common code of her society is a valuable one and she benefits from it as an artist. Mr. Knightley's speech to Emma, reproving her for snubbing Miss Bates, is a useful instance: manners there are seen to be based on moral values. Mrs. Wharton's worthy people are all primitives or archaic survivals. This inability to find any significance in the society that she spent her prime in, or to find "significance only through what its frivolity destroys," explains the absence of poetry in her disposition and of many kinds of valuable experience in her books. She has none of that natural piety, that richness of feeling and sense of a moral order, of experience as a process of growth, in which George Eliot's local criticisms are embedded and which give the latter her large stature. Between her conviction that the new society she grew up into was vicious and insecurely based on an ill-used working class and her conviction that her inherited mode of living represented a dead end, she could find no foundation to build on. We may see where her real strength lay in the critical phrases she uses: "Her moral muscles had become atrophied [by buying off suffering with money, or denying its existence with words]"; "the superficial contradictions and accommodations of a conscience grown elastic from too much use"—and in the short story "Autres Temps . . ." a study of the change in moral codes she had witnessed since her youth. Here the divorced mother, who had for many years hidden her disgrace in Florence, returns to America to succor, as she thinks, her divorced and newly remarried daughter. At first, finding the absence of any prejudice against divorce in the new America, she is exalted, then she feels in her bewilderment " 'I didn't take up much room before, but now where is there a corner for me?' . . . Where indeed in this crowded, topsy-turvey world, with its headlong changes and helter-skelter readjustments, its new tolerances and indifferences and accommodations, was there room for a character fashioned by slower sterner processes and a life broken under their inexorable pressure?" And finally, depressed by what she feels to be the lack of any kind of moral taste, she loses her illusions about the real benefits of such a change, she finds it to be merely a change in social fashions and not a revolution bringing genuine enlightenment based on good feeling. She explains to an old friend: " 'Traditions that have lost their meaning are the hardest of all to destroy. . . . We're shut up in a little tight round of habit and association, just as we're shut up in this room. . . . We're all imprisoned, of course—all of us middling people, who don't carry freedom in our brains. But we've accommodated ourselves to our different cells, and if we're moved suddenly into new ones we're likely to find a stone wall where we thought there was air, and to knock ourselves senseless against it.' " She chooses to return to Florence, "moving again among the grim edges of reality."

Mrs. Wharton, if unfortunate in her environment, had a strength of character that made her superior to it. She was a remarkable novelist if not a large-sized one, and while there are few great novelists there are not even so many remarkable ones that we can afford to let her be overlooked.

Edith Wharton

by Alfred Kazin

It is easy to say now that Edith Wharton's great subject should have been the biography of her own class, for her education and training had given her alone in her literary generation the best access to it. But the very significance of that education was her inability to transcend and use it. Since she could do no other, she chose instead to write, in various forms and with unequal success, the one story she knew best, the story that constituted her basic experience—her own. Her great theme, like that of her friend Henry James, became the plight of the young and innocent in a world of greater intricacy than they were accustomed to. But where James was obsessed by the moral complexity of that theme and devoted his career to the evaluation and dramatization of opposing cultures, (Edith Wharton specialized in tales of victimization.) To James the emotional problems of his characters were the representative expression of a larger world of speech, manners, and instinct —whose significance was psychological and universal. He saw his work as a body of problems that tested the novelist's capacity for difficulty and responsibility. To Edith Wharton, whose very career as a novelist was the tenuous product of so many personal maladjustments, the novel became an involuted expression of self.)

She was too cultivated, too much the patrician all her days, to vulgarize or even to simplify the obvious relations between her life and her work; she was too fastidious an artist even in her constricted sphere to yield to that obvious romanticism which fulfills itself in explicit confession. But fundamentally she had to fall back upon her-

"Edith Wharton." From *On Native Grounds*, by Alfred Kazin (New York: Harcourt, Brace, & World, Inc., 1942). One section of the chapter "Edith Wharton and Theodore Dreiser." Copyright 1942 by Alfred Kazin. Reprinted by permission of Harcourt, Brace, & World, Inc.

self, since she was never, as she well knew, to rise above the personal difficulties that attended her career. She escaped the tedium and mediocrity to which her class had condemned her, but the very motivation of that escape was to become a great artist, to attain by the extension of her powers the liberation she needed as a woman; and a great artist, even a completely devoted artist, she never became. James, who gave her friendship, could encourage but not instruct her. Actually, it was not to become such a writer as he, but to become a writer, that she struggled; what he had to give her—(precision of motive, cultivation of taste, the sense of style—she possessed by disposition and training) James's need of art was urgent, but its urgency was of the life of the spirit; Edith Wharton's was desperate, and by a curious irony she escaped that excessive refinement and almost abstract mathematical passion for art that encumbered James. She could speak out plainly with a force he could never muster; her own alienation and loneliness gave her a sympathy for erratic spirits and "illicit" emotions that was unique in its time. It has been forgotten how much Edith Wharton contributed to the plain-speaking traditions of American realism. Women wrote to her indignantly asking if she had known respectable women; Charles Eliot Norton once even warned her that "no great work of the imagination has ever been based on illicit passion."

The greater consequence of Edith Wharton's failure to fulfill herself in art was its deepening of her innate disposition to tragedy. She was conscious of that failure even when she was most successful, and in the gap between her resolution and her achievement she had recourse to a classical myth, the pursuing Eumenides who will not let Lily Bart—or Edith Wharton—rest. She was among the few in her generation to attain the sense of tragedy, even the sense of the world as pure evil, and it found expression in the biting edge of her novels and the superficially genial fatalism of their drama. "Life is the saddest thing," she wrote once, "next to death," and the very simplicity and purity of that knowledge set her off in a literary generation to whom morality signified the fervor of the muckrakers and for whom death as a philosophical issue had no meaning. Spiritually, indeed, Edith Wharton was possessed of resources so much finer than any contemporary American novelist could muster that even the few superior novelists of her time seem

gross by comparison. It was a service, even though, like so many
artistic services, it was an unconscious one, to talk the language of
the soul at a time when the best energies in American prose were
devoted to the complex new world of industrial capitalism.

Yet what a subject lay before Edith Wharton in that world, if
only she had been able, or willing, to use it! Her class was dying
slowly but not painfully, and it was passing on into another existence. To write that story she would have had to tell bluntly how
her class had yielded to the *novi homines* of the Gilded Age, how
it had sold itself joyfully, given over its houses, married off its ac-
quiescent daughters, and in the end—like all bourgeois aristocracies
—asserted itself in the new dominion of power under the old standard of family and caste. It would have been the immemorial tale of
aristocrat and merchant in a capitalist society, their mating, their
mutual accommodation, their reconciliation. Edith Wharton knew
that story well enough; its significance had sundered the only world
she knew, and its victims were to crowd her novels. The fastidious
college lawyers who had scorned the methods of a Daniel Drew in
the Seventies would do the work of a Carnegie in the Nineties; the
Newport settled first by the Whartons and their friends was now to
become the great summer resort of the frontier-bred plutocracy; the
New York that had crystallized around the houses and reputations
of the Livingstons, the Crugers, the Schuylers, the Waltons, now gave
room to the Vanderbilts, whose family crest might properly have
been the prow of a ferryboat on a field gilded with Erie Railroad
bonds, with the imperishable boast of its Commodore founder for
a motto: "Law! What do I care about law? Hain't I got the power?"
So had the eighteenth century Dukes of Nottingham developed the
mines on their hereditary estates; so would the seedy marquises of
France under the Third Republic marry American sewing-machine
heiresses. Howells had said it perfectly: the archetype of the new era
was "the man who has risen." To tell that story as Edith Wharton
might have told it would have involved the creation of a monumen-
tal tragicomedy, for was not the aristocracy from which she stemmed
as fundamentally middle-class as the rising tide of capitalists out
of the West it was prepared to resist?

Edith Wharton knew well enough that one dynasty had succeeded
another in American life; the consequences of that succession be-

came the great subject of her best novels. But she was not so much interested in the accession of the new class as she was in the destruction of her own, in the eclipse of its finest spirits. Like Lily Bart, Ellen Olenska, Ralph Marvell, she too was one of its fine spirits; and she translated effortlessly and pointedly the difficulties of her own career into the difficulties of young aristocrats amid a hostile and alien culture. It is the aristocrat yielding, the aristocrat suffering, who bestrides her best novels: the sensitive cultivated castaways who are either destroyed by their own class or tied by marriage or need to the vulgar nouveaux riches. Henry James could write of revolutionaries and nobility, painters and politicians, albeit all talked the Jamesian language with the same aerial remoteness from plain speech; Edith Wharton's imagination was obsessed by the fellow spirits of her youth. Though she had been hurt by her class and had made her career by escaping its fundamental obligations, she could not, despite all her fertile powers of invention, conceive of any character who was not either descended from that class or placed in some obvious and dramatic relation to it. At bottom she could love only those who, like herself, had undergone a profound alienation but were inextricably bound to native loyalties and taste. Indeed, their very weakness endeared them to her: to rise in the industrial-capitalist order was to succumb to its degradations. "Why do we call our generous ideas illusions, and the mean ones truth?" cries Lawrence Selden in *The House of Mirth*. It was Edith Wharton's stricken cry. She had accepted all the conditions of servitude to the vulgar new order save the obligation to respect its values. Yet it was in the very nature of things that she should rebel not by adopting a new set of values or by interesting herself in a new society, but by resigning herself to soundless heroism. Thus she could read in the defeat of her characters the last proud affirmation of the caste quality. If failure was the destiny of superior men and women in the modern world, failure was the mark of spiritual victory. For that is what Edith Wharton's sense of tragedy came to in the end; she could conceive of no society but her own, she could not live with what she had. Doom waited for the pure in heart; and it was better so.

Is not that the theme of *Ethan Frome* as well as of *The House of Mirth*? Ethan, like Lily Bart or Ralph Marvell, fails because he is spiritually superior and materially useless; he has been loyal to one set of values, one conception of happiness, but powerless before the obligations of his society. It was not a New England story and certainly not the granite "folk tale" of New England *in esse* its admirers have claimed it to be. She knew little of the New England common world, and perhaps cared even less; the story was begun as an exercise in French while she was living in Lenox, Massachusetts, and she wanted a simple frame and "simple" characters. The world of the Frome tragedy is abstract. She never knew how the poor lived in Paris or London; she knew even less of how they lived in the New England villages where she spent an occasional summer. There is indeed nothing in any of her work, save perhaps the one notable story she wrote of people who work for a living, *The Bunner Sisters*, to indicate that she had any conception of the tensions and responsibilities of even the most genteel middle-class poverty. Sympathy she possessed by the very impulse of her imagination, but it was a curious sympathy which assumed that if life in her own class was often dreary, the world "below" must be even more so. Whenever she wrote of that world, darkness and revulsion entered her work mechanically. She thought of the poor not as a class but as a condition; the qualities she automatically ascribed to the poor—drabness, meanness, anguish—became another manifestation of the futility of human effort.

Edith Wharton was not confined to that darkness; she could hate, and hate hard, but the object of her hatred was the emerging new class of brokers and industrialists, the makers and promoters of the industrial era who were beginning to expropriate and supplant her own class. She disliked them no less fiercely than did the rebellious novelists of the muckrake era—the Robert Herricks, the David Graham Phillipses, the Upton Sinclairs; but where these novelists saw in the brokers and industrialists a new and supreme condition in American society, Edith Wharton seemed to be personally affronted by them. It is the grande dame, not the objective novelist, who speaks out in her caricatures of Rosedale and Undine Spragg. To the women of the new class she gave names like Looty Arlington and Indiana Frusk; to their native habitats, names like Pruneville, Nebraska, and Halleluja, Missouri. She had no conception of America as a unified and dynamic economy, or even as a single culture. There was old New York, the great house in Lenox (from which she gazed down upon Ethan Frome), and the sprawling wilderness that called itself the Middle West, a land of graceless manners, hoary jests, businessmen, and ridiculous provincial speech. It was a condescending resignation that evoked in her the crackling irony that smarted in her prose; it was the biting old dowager of American letters who snapped at her lower-class characters and insulted them so roundly that her very disgust was comic. As the world about her changed beyond all recognition, she ignored the parvenu altogether and sought refuge in nostalgia. Her social views, never too liberal or expansive, now solidified themselves into the traditional views of reaction. After 1920, when she had fulfilled her debt to the past with *The Age of Innocence*, she lost even that interest in the craft of fiction which had singled her out over the years, and with mechanical energy poured out a series of cheap novels which, with their tired and forlorn courtesy, their smooth rendering of the smooth problems of women's magazine fiction, suggest that Edith Wharton exhausted herself periodically, and then finally, because she had so quickly exhausted the need that drove her to literature.

If it is curious to remember that she always suggested more distinction than she possessed, it is even more curious to see how the interests of the American novel have since passed her by. James has the recurrent power to excite the literary mind. Edith Wharton, who believed so passionately in the life of art that she staked her life upon it, remains not a great artist but an unusual American, one who brought the weight of her personal experience to bear upon a modern American literature to which she was spiritually alien.

Edith Wharton: The Art of the Novel

by E. K. Brown

How far a high and original creative talent can accommodate itself to the rôle of disciple is evidenced in the interesting case of Edith Wharton. To Henry James, "almost the only novelist who has formulated his ideas about his art," Mrs. Wharton's debt is almost incomputably great. To his theory and practice of the craft of fiction, she owes what is surest and finest in her technique; and, moreover, many of her individual works would not be just what they are, were it not for certain strangely similar works of Henry James. The trifocal presentation of the tale in *Twilight Sleep*—with its three focal characters members of one family and inmates of one New York house—is in a fine sense a later version of *Washington Square* where the focal characters are in the same relation to one another. The picture of the Faubourg Saint Germain in *Madame de Treymes* owes as much to *The American* and *Madame de Mauves* as it does to direct observation. The mode in which Kate Clephane's problem in *The Mother's Recompense* is put before her takes the critical reader back to thread the more tortuous complexities of *The Golden Bowl*. From beginning to end *The Reef* is Jamesian: it is inconceivable that this novel would have its special virtue if Henry James had not developed his later manner.

Henry James twitted Mrs. Wharton on her admiration for George Eliot, "perhaps born with the richest gifts of any English novelist since Thackeray," and her resemblances to "that most excellent woman," as he demurely called her. To less perceptive eyes than his a comparison between the two suggested itself in the superficial

Edith Wharton: "The Art of the Novel." From *The Art of the Novel*, by Pelham Edgar (New York: The Macmillan Company, 1933). Reprinted by permission of Mrs. E. K. Brown.

but striking likeness between *The Valley of Decision* and *Romola*. Even if these two novels were fundamentally alike, the relation established between Mrs. Wharton and George Eliot would be slight, for *The Valley of Decision* is altogether unlike Mrs. Wharton's other works. It is clearly off-center. Where she most significantly resembles George Eliot is in her ability—an ability she has had from the beginning—to transcend the limitation of her sex. Like George Eliot, she is at ease in a man's world. When she narrates in the first person, the narrator is in almost every case a man. She carries off her men to Abner Spragg's office or to Newland Archer's library or to John Campton's studio and they are as vivid, as characteristic, as genuine as in a drawing room or a summerhouse. In two technical respects she is greatly George Eliot's superior. She has liberated herself from "the purely artificial necessity of the double plot." Throughout the novels of Dickens, George Eliot, Trollope and the majority of their contemporaries, "this tedious and senseless convention persists, checking the progress of each series of events and distracting the reader's attention." Mrs. Wharton was too astute a pupil of Balzac, Flaubert, and Turgenev to let such a convention pass unquestioned. She permits no bifurcation of interest in her fiction, no parallelism of development.

She finds fault with George Eliot on a second count of "continually pausing to denounce and exhort." It is not the morality, but the crudity of its presentation which repels her. For she too is profoundly and pertinaciously occupied with moral issues: her morality is not excrescent but inherent. George Eliot goes to the middle class for the substance of her best works; and in temper her work is middle-class. But widely as Mrs. Wharton's fiction differs from hers in substance and temper, their presuppositions are the same—a constituted social order of which each individual is a part and may be a center, a civilization and a culture against which heroic individuals must rebel but will be grievously wounded in rebelling, a morality which emerges from the social order and the civilization and cannot be imposed upon it.

"The two central difficulties of the novel," says Mrs. Wharton, "have to do with the choice of the point from which the subject is to be seen, and with the attempt to produce on the reader the effect of the passage of time." On the matter of time, Henry James, Mr.

Percy Lubbock and Mrs. Wharton have written often and at some
length; but the matter is so intractable that none of the three has
made much of it. With the other matter, "the question of the point
of view—the question of the relation in which the narrator stands
to the story," as Mr. Lubbock formulates it, they have been more
successful than any other theorists of fiction.

It may almost be said that Mrs. Wharton begins where Mr. Lubbock leaves off or—to put it more equitably—that Mr. Lubbock
gives us the schema of a theorist and Mrs. Wharton the comments
and counsels of a practitioner. Mr. Lubbock's principal conclusion
is the supreme value of "the story that is centered in somebody's
consciousness, passed through a fashioned and constituted mind—
not poured straight into the book from the mind of the author,
which is a far-away matter, vaguely divined, with no certain edge to
it." A "fashioned" story he finds to be "of stronger stuff than a simple
and undramatic report." The whole of his great book, *The Craft of
Fiction,* may be considered a preparation, illustration, and elaboration of that conclusion.

That conclusion Mrs. Wharton assumes; and she contents herself
with indicating the difficulties inherent for the craftsman in the
method of narration through "reflecting consciousnesses." Is it
better tactics, she inquires—and this is her most important addition
to Mr. Lubbock's investigation—for the novelist to limit himself to
one center of vision, to one focal character, or should he permit the
center of vision to shift "from one character to another, in such a
way as to comprehend the whole history and yet preserve the unity
of impression?" "It is best," she says, "to shift as seldom as possible,
and to let the tale work itself out from not more than two (or at most
three) angles of vision, choosing as reflecting consciousnesses persons
either in close mental and moral relation to each other, or discern-
ing enough to estimate each other's parts in the drama, so that the
latter, even viewed from different angles, always presents itself to
the reader *as a whole.*" It is implicit in this formula, I think, that
Mrs. Wharton sees no virtue whatever in the multiplication of focal
characters—for her, two are better than three and one is better than
two. Such a novel as Mr. Hergesheimer's *Java Head* with its ten
angles of vision, or such a poetic fiction as *The Ring and The Book*
with ten and the author's own, would seem to her to impose an

illicit strain upon the reader. I have quoted Mr. Lubbock's remark
that the focal novel is superior to the nonfocal because it has been
"passed through a fashioned and constituted mind"; and what it
gains in such a passing is unity of tone and definiteness of outline—
harmony and proportion. But if parts of the novel have been passed
through one mind and other parts through another, how can the
whole acquire the desiderated harmony and proportion? They may
be acquired, Mrs. Wharton points out, if the reflecting consciousnesses are in "close mental and moral relation to each other," ap-
proximating, that is to say, a unity. *The Reef* is an exquisite example
of such a relation: there is no strain, no harassing process of readjust-
ing one's vision when the reader turns from the consciousness of
Anne to go behind the character of Darrow. *Hudson River
Bracketed,* with the shift from Vance to Halo, is a more audacious
enterprise: at their first meeting the gap between them is huge, and
in the early chapters of the novel there is a distinctly perceptible
strain in shifting one's vision. When there are three focal characters,
as in *Twilight Sleep*—three characters of quite unrelated intelli-
gences and emotions although they are father, mother, and daughter
—there is no marked harmony or proportion. The novel would lose
little and gain much if it were direct narrative. The closeness of
moral relation between Lily Bart and Lawrence Selden saves *The
House of Mirth* from so harsh a verdict; but Gerty Farish, the third
focal character, is hopelessly disparate from them, and to see either
of them from her point of vision is to imperil the wholeness of her
conception of them; and to make matters worse, we are permitted
occasional peeps into the consciousness of still a fourth character,
Lily's aunt, a character as remote from Lily and Lawrence as from
Gerty.

In the greater novels of her middle years—in *The House of Mirth,
The Reef,* and *Ethan Frome*—Mrs. Wharton practiced with the
happiest result her creed of economy in dialogue. It would be difficult to exceed her economic skill in *The Reef* where she uses very
freely the long intricate unspoken soliloquy so dear to the later
Henry James. If she is less economical of dialogue in her later novels,
there is compensation in her steadily growing art for revealing character in conversation. She has cunningly diversified her very turn of
sentence to bring out what is at once significant and peculiar in the

speaker. With almost any New Yorker she always succeeds, whether her personage be aristocrat, pseudoaristocrat or plutocrat, conventional or individual, dainty or robust or florid, old or young, man or woman. With her New Englanders also she succeeds—with the farmers in *Ethan Frome* and the villagers and outcasts in *Summer,* with the Bostonian Adelaide Painter in *The Reef.* With her French characters—notably those in *A Son at the Front* and *The Custom of the Country*—she is so excellent as to have no English or American superior unless it be Conrad in *Lord Jim.* Her competence is no less when she represents the speech of Americans whose spiritual home is Europe: from *Madame de Treymes* to *The Children* she has illuminated them in their conversation, and a very fair measure of her success with Ellen Olenska (née Mingott) issues from dialogue. She has made herself the accomplished mistress of the modes and syncopated rhythms of speech which have developed since the war; and these she employs with aptness and accuracy in *Twilight Sleep, The Children,* and *Hudson River Bracketed.*

Commenting (in *The Bookman,* May, 1905), on Mr. Howard Sturgis's novel *Belchamber,* at a time when *The House of Mirth* must have been in the foreground of her mind, Mrs. Wharton wrote: "A handful of vulgar people, bent only on spending and enjoying, may seem a negligible factor in the social development of the race; but they become an engine of destruction through the illusions they kill and the generous ardor they turn to despair." Replace the words "generous ardor"—which are apt for Lord Belchamber rather than for Lily Bart—by "genuine aspiration" and you have the formula of *The House of Mirth* and the temper in which it was written. It speaks well for the discrimination of 1905 and 1906 that so pungent a social criticism, so acrid a tragedy, so shapely a work of art, should have been a best seller.

Despite Mrs. Wharton's endeavor to narrate with serene objectivity the encounter of Lily Bart with the forces of society, one feels from beginning to end that there is a prisoner in the dock. It is not the "captured dryad" as Mrs. Wharton calls Lily more than once: it is not even the collection of social mountaineers against which she is pitted. It is—to borrow the title of one of Mrs. Wharton's later novels—"the custom of the country." It was the custom of the country that led the smart set of New York to be complacent accomplices in the wrecking of a life which was, however uncertainly, a life given to a quest for beauty.

Few books can have so surprised an author's public as did *Ethan Frome* in 1911. For more than a decade Mrs. Wharton's fiction had dealt exclusively with metropolitan and cosmopolitan society, with a world whose pivots were money and luxury and art and beauty; with each passing year she had proved herself more and more the novelist of civilization; yet in *Ethan Frome* she accomplished something as bleak and simple as a sketch of Sarah Orne Jewett. It was as bewildering as if Henry James had written of the villagers of Rye or Mr. Cabell of the Negroes of Richmond.

There is no question that *Ethan Frome* is of all Mrs. Wharton's works the most certain to endure. One can go further: there is nothing in the work of Henry James or of W. D. Howells that has a better chance of survival. Eleven years after its first publication, in her introduction to the reprint of *Ethan Frome* in *The Modern Students' Library*, Mrs. Wharton frankly said: "It was the first subject I had ever approached with full confidence in its value, for my own purpose, and a relative faith in my power to render at least a part of what I saw in it." Her faith and confidence were not misplaced. The only significant reader who found it a disappointment was Henry James.

It is probable that what disappointed Henry James was the peculiar organization of the novelette, perhaps, too, the fact that it was a novelette rather than a novel. Of her decision to confine the story to a novelette Mrs. Wharton says:

> The problem before me, as I saw in the first flash, was this: I had to deal with a subject of which the dramatic climax, or rather the anti-climax, occurs a generation later than the first acts of the tragedy. This enforced lapse of time would seem to anyone persuaded—as I have always been—that every subject (in the novelist's sense of the term) implicitly *contains its own form and dimension,* to mark Ethan Frome as the subject for a novel. But I never thought this for a moment, for I had felt, at the same time, that the theme of my tale was not one on which many variations could be played. It must be treated as starkly and summarily as life had always presented itself to my protagonists: any attempt to elaborate or complicate their sentiments would necessarily have falsified the whole. They were, in truth, those

figures, *my granite outcroppings;* but half-emerged from the soil and scarcely more articulate.

In a word the evolution of the novelette is abrupt, jagged, truncated to emphasize the granitic inarticulate quality of its characters. It is not a novel because its characters are not fluent or complex to the degree that the novel requires. How firmly Mrs. Wharton is convinced of the propriety of the novelette form for such a theme and such a type of character is shown by her restriction of *Summer,* her only other New England story of any length, to the dimension approved for *Ethan Frome.* The perfect air of reality in these stories is the product of the most cunning and deliberate art.

The House of Mirth is at once a studied portrait of a single character and a sketch of the manners of a versatile and numerous group —sometimes indeed the division of interest perturbs an avid reader and may even lead him to doubt the clearness of the intuition from which the novel issues. In *The Reef,* published in 1912, there is no such division. "The problem which Mrs. Wharton at last reached in *The Reef,*" says Mr. Percy Lubbock, "is that of the squarely faced, intently studied portrait; and the portrait she produced is surely, on the whole, the most compellingly beautiful thing in all her work." One assents to Henry James's comment, more apposite to the last book than to any other part of the novel, that "there remains with one so strongly the impression of its quality and of the unspeakably *fouillé* nature of the situation between the two principals (more gone into and with more undeviating truth than anything you have done). . . ." One assents, but not without a perception that, as Professor Lovett says, the novel dwindles into a chronicle of purely intramental events, sacrificing as Henry James was glad to do, the values of dramatic impact for those of psychological elaboration. One's estimate of *The Reef* is deeply engaged in one's estimate of *The Ambassadors, The Wings of the Dove,* and *The Golden Bowl.* It is Mrs. Wharton's greatest discipular work.

Mrs. Wharton's friendly admiration for Roosevelt is well known: to his memory she wrote the most moving of her elegies. The principle of her social criticism is not far removed from the better principles of his social action. She would relate the life of the aristocrats of New York to the life of the nation, stirring in them a sense of social responsibility. She would relate it also to the intellectual and artistic life of the world, committing these aristocrats to a vast general culture and a response to aesthetic stimulation keen enough and sure enough to guide the nation and contribute to the guidance of the world. She would broaden and deepen and diversify the currents of aristocratic life so that instead of the "innocence" of the Seventies or the animality of the Twenties there should be conscience and balance. In a word she would make of the aristocracy of New York what the hopeful imagination of Henry James made of the aristocracy of England and the American expatriates—she would make of it a world of Chad Newsomes and Milly Theales. The mention of Henry James suggests his wish that Mrs. Wharton should be tethered in her own backyard; that backyard was the aristocratic life of New York. It is about that backyard that she has written her most significant social criticism, of aristocrats and for aristocrats to be sure, but in a mood of scarcely stifled rage against their complacency in weakness and ease.

No other American aristocrat has addressed the members of his class in such a mood. Indeed it is not easy to find an analogue to Mrs. Wharton's mood anywhere. One thinks of Thackeray only to remember how often his incurable sentimentality deflects the aim of his satire and negates the apparent intention of his social criticism. The early novels of Jane Austen are comparable; but the staid authoress of *Mansfield Park* would not have repeated the satires of her youth—her respect for religion would have deterred her from drawing another Mr. Collins and her respect for the gentry would have shrunk from the audacity of conceiving another Lady Catherine. And the satire of Jane Austen is purely devastating: no ideal is implicit in its sneers. One must, as in so many other places, go outside English fiction to find a kindred body of work. Turgenev is perhaps the true analogue for Mrs. Wharton: in *Rudin,* in *A Month in the Country,* in *Fathers and Sons*—to name but three of his books—is to be found the same kind of intelligence, addressing itself in the same kind of medium, to the same kind of task. Henry James was not the only American novelist who "went abroad and read Turgenev."

The House of Mirth Revisited

by Diana Trilling

It was in 1905, at the age of forty-three, that Edith Wharton published her remarkable novel of upper-class life in New York, *The House of Mirth,* the book that first proclaimed her literary stature. Even at the height of her fame and powers, Mrs. Wharton was acutely aware of the ever-widening distance between the world in which she had been reared and the general movement of American society as it was developing around her; her autobiography, *A Backward Glance,* which appeared in 1934, is a reminiscence deeply informed with melancholy recognition of the new conditions that barred her from full participation in the experience of her times. But the vast social changes Mrs. Wharton reported in her memoir were of course minor compared with the revolutionary alterations that have followed her death in 1937. Another quarter-century has delivered the mortal blow to the society in which she came of literary age, so that it is small wonder that her extraordinary work has passed into the archeological shadows and that now, where she is known at all outside university English courses, it is merely, and pejoratively, as a society lady become society author. Today, if we attach meaning to her name it is likely to be only that which lies in what we are pleased to call her snobbery—her pride of birth, her delicate skirting of the common life, her addiction to an outmoded social protocol. Even the fresh critical light which belatedly revealed the fierce moral passion of Henry James has not yet penetrated the obscurity of his "Dearest Edith," his long-time friend and colleague. It still remains for criticism to show Mrs. Wharton in her proper place in the main stream of American literature.

Our picture of an embattled aristocrat cultivating her private garden behind a high wall of reticence and social fastidiousness is as little consistent, however, with Mrs. Wharton's work as the old genteel image of James was with his. Although there is little doubt that in her personal life Edith Wharton held fast to the privileges of her class, it is anything but the case that her creative powers were in the service of a social vision defined by the presuppositions of that class. The way of the artist is a strange one; in Mrs. Wharton's instance, the mysterious process by which a lifetime's deference to the imperatives of birth and social position was transformed into a driving literary concern with moral truth will perhaps never yield its whole explanation.

The proud descendant of Rhinelanders and Gallatins, who could recall but one person "in trade" who had ever been received in her home, who enclosed her calling card with the manuscripts of her first poems, and who sadly lamented the passing of a day when the gentlemen of her acquaintance were available for social intercourse in the afternoon no less than in the evening hours because none of them worked; the writer living in France who would suffer no taint of the Left Bank and divided her residence between the rue de Varennes and an eighteenth century chateau whose servants addressed each other as *Monsieur* and *Madame*—such a person would appear little suited to the freemasonry of literature. But this is precisely the point about Edith Wharton: her commitment to the democratic principle, if it can be said to have existed at all, existed only in a much transmogrified form. She was in social actuality the aristocrat that all literary artists are, and must be, in spirit—however strenuously they deny the social concretization of their personal "difference." She saw no reason to assimilate herself to the generality of mankind in order to validate her right to deal with man's fate in society; on the contrary, she assumed (or at least never questioned the fact) that to have one's own firm social base from which to examine man in society was to operate with a distinct advantage as an artist. And this was indeed how it worked out. Her social position enabled her not merely to bring the fact of high society into literature in all its concreteness and authenticity—this was the least of her achievements—but also made it uniquely possible for her to perceive the complex and subtle interplay between our personal destinies and the destiny foredained by our particular social situation.

Fortified as she was in her own class, she knew the reality of class as no theoretical Marxist or social egalitarian can know it: not speculatively but in her bones. The captive, in her private life, of the values that accrue to a social group which is as firmly based in economic power as in lineage, she knew that the differences between rich and poor, between the socially protected and the socially vulnerable, are more than mere forms or illusions, that they are the realest of realities. The insight into social truth that the novelist usually generates out of his own imagination Mrs. Wharton achieved by, so to speak, social right. And she exercised it on behalf of a moral earnestness in no way the less reliable for being so entirely alien to the predatory world with which she had her closest association.

Today, in our approach to fiction, we persistently overlook this paradox: that the writer who may appear to be least concerned with social or political renovation often has most to say for the social good. While we no longer apply the primitive criteria of the Thirties, when the novel had to be justified by its usefulness in the class war that was believed to be imminent, we still require the novelist to take his stand well outside the socially given, at some point where we can be sure he shares our protest against an unsatisfactory social organization. In the measure that we feel overwhelmed by the political problems of our time, which Marxism failed to solve for us, we reject any effort of social particularization, conceiving it to be, in all likelihood, the beginning of a bias which will lead to untruthfulness. It is as if our failure to have waged successful class war in the Thirties now makes it mandatory that we deny any reality of class, any distinctions of social topography, or, certainly, any healthy conjunction between a writer's place in society and his moral vision.

Looked at in this light, *The House of Mirth* can hardly be expected to give satisfaction, for it is nothing if not a novel about social stratification and the consequences of breaking the taboos of class. In addition, its author is in important part identified with the distinctly upper-case Society which she is putting under such rigorous inspection—and this is not merely a matter of what we know of her life, it has also to do with where Mrs. Wharton locates herself in relation to the story she tells. Writing of Lily Bart, a beautiful young woman fated to destruction because she violated the laws of her social group, Mrs. Wharton never renounces her community with Lily's harsh judges, not even when she is exposing their most vicious hypocrisies. Her attack is always within the family. *The House of Mirth* is nevertheless one of the most telling indictments of a social system based on the chance distribution of wealth, and therefore of social privilege, that has ever been put on paper. Indeed, what accounts for its extraordinary moral texture no less than its complex accuracy as a piece of social reporting is Mrs. Wharton's simultaneous acceptance of the social group into which she was born and her unflinching confrontation of the evils it perpetrates.

At the turn of the century, which is the period of *The House of Mirth,* Mrs. Wharton's social class had already begun to feel the assaults that in our own day have spelled the disappearance of its once-unquestioned sense of power. Inherited wealth had begun to capitulate to new financial success; infiltrations from an uneasy European aristocracy and from the freer lands of the theater and art had already presaged our present-day international set. The solvent was at work within even the innermost circles of hereditary privilege, preparing the democratic integration and the mobility between classes with which we are now familiar.

One counts several carefully differentiated strata of New York Society in Mrs. Wharton's novel—the Proustian precision with which these dividing lines are drawn is not the least of the fascinations of the book. But it is not so much in their differences—the fact, say, that the Dorset-Trenor circle takes it for granted that ladies smoke and gamble, while the Gryce-Van Osburgh-Peniston circle countenances no such impropriety—as in their shared weaknesses that we read the impending collapse of the whole precious structure. If the conservatives of Society feel threatened by Dorsets and Trenors who no longer adhere to the rules by which they were reared, these "faster" members of their class are similarly aware of the new forces beating at *their* gate and the new values to which they are soon to be exposed; no segment of Society but knows it is imperiled by the large movement of social change. And although in isolated personal instances there may be a certain flexibility in response to the disturbance of old patterns, there is no class flexibility with which to accommodate a new order. Nor is there, of course, an adequate inflexibility or intransigence with which to resist it; there cannot be, unless this world of privilege marshal its strength to destroy the insurgent democratic horde—an act of militant counter-assertion, actually of counter-revolution, which society is already too decadent even to envision. What Mrs. Wharton is describing, in other words, is the inexorable process of history as it worked itself out in the America with which she was best acquainted.

An artist fiercely in possession of her own particular materials, Mrs. Wharton only once—and this once rather deplorably—undertakes to introduce into her novel the encroaching democratic mass which constitutes the palpable or, at any rate, the ultimate social enemy. This is when Lily Bart, nearing the climax of her short career, encounters a working-class girl whose path she had crossed in a vagrant moment of personal philanthropy. For the rest, Mrs. Wharton's representative of the new social dispensation is a Jew, a very rich Jew, Simon Rosedale, who is intent upon making a marriage which will fittingly ornament his enormous wealth and ensure him a place in Society. Not only the innermost circles but even the outlying sections of the old aristocratic world are at first resistant to Rosedale's intrusion; but they are unable to withstand the power of his money, and his urgency of personal ambition. This most alien of Mrs. Wharton's characters at last penetrates the central strongholds; and if his worldly success coincides with the steady revelation of a far more feeling nature than showed in the days when he was failing so dismally in his social effort, we can take this as not the least pointed of Mrs. Wharton's comments on the connection between social realities and the life of the emotions. Obviously Mrs. Wharton is not saying that an achieved position in Society is the warrant of good feelings: her panorama of Lily's brutally shallow and callous friends argues quite the opposite. But she surely is saying that our gentler emotions have a hard time thriving when we lack a sense of our secure niche in the world, whatever it may be, or, as in Lily's case, without the nourishment of money.

The historical moment, then, of *The House of Mirth* is the mo-

ment when a Jew—and a self-made Jew at that, uncouth and charm-
less, whose deviations from accepted deportment are as conspicuous
as his wealth and as grating on the sensitive nerve of Society—can
aspire to associate on equal terms with the old Hudson Valley
families. But this is still the moment when the old social monarchs,
aware that a new dynasty of wealth storms the inherited realm, cling
most tenaciously to their rights of blood; the struggle is the fiercer
because eventually so futile. Through most of *The House of Mirth*
Rosedale takes social and personal insult to a degree that would
flatten any except a man of iron will—except a man, that is, whose
personal will was synonymous with the will of history. His strength
of endurance lies in his awareness that it is only so long as the old
fortunes hold out that the old families can maintain their prestige
and power, and in his sure knowledge that his own shrewd speculations on Wall Street are in the process of blasting their hereditary
fortress.

It is into this world of wealth and privilege, much shaken but still
unyielding, that Mrs. Wharton's heroine has been born just short of
thirty years before the novel opens. Living wildly beyond their
limited means, Lily Bart's parents had never had more than a
perilous foothold in New York Society; now they are dead, bank-
rupt, and therefore forgotten, and they have left their daughter
to the half-hearted care of a widowed aunt, Mrs. Peniston, a cold,
self-centered bastion of respectability. Determined to survive where
her parents had perished, Lily has a single course open to her: she
must make the marriage for which she has been groomed and for
which she is so well qualified by her beauty and charm. But even
as the story opens, there is the sure premonition of disaster. Lily
is already 29, and has missed her best chances. She has become the
perennial guest of wealth, moving from one great country house
to another, dutifully smoothing her way with small services to her
busy hostesses. At heart, she is unamenable to the social group in
which she seeks establishment; she zigzags disastrously between the
most gifted conformity to the behavior required of a young woman
in search of a rich, well-placed husband and sudden impulses which
run dangerously counter to the commands of practical reason.

Although Lily's departures from convention represent a natural
superiority to her social group, she lacks the money and family back-

ing to support her divergence, and she also lacks the harsh consistency without which rebellion is exposed as a weakness. In a predatory world, to give the least sign of faltering is to invite annihilation, and we watch Lily move to her downfall. When she is pressed with debts she allows Gus Trenor, the husband of her closest friend, to make investments for her; it is his own money Trenor advances, and Lily is deeply compromised. She crosses the amatory field of the frenetic Mrs. Dorset, provoking that powerful lady's hostility. In crucial moments of her marital campaigns she offends her few remaining prospects by neglecting them in favor of Lawrence Selden, a bachelor of only modest means. Blundering and miscalculating but constantly growing in moral stature, Lily meets her inevitable end—poverty, ostracism by relatives and friends, death.

It is clear that what Mrs. Wharton is captured by in Lily Bart is her ambiguity of purpose, the conflict between her practical good sense and the pull of spirit. And what makes Lily a heroine for the reader—one of the greatly appealing heroines of fiction, worthy of association with Emma Bovary and Anna Karenina—is the ultimate triumph of spirit over good sense, even though the transcendence guarantees her destruction. Were Lily's spirit more in tune with her society, the novel might have ended with her practical victory over the poor souls who surround her, but the achievement would make her no better a creation than they. On the other hand, it is a mistake to think of Lily as Mrs. Wharton's model of virtuousness. She is "pure" neither in her own nor her author's eyes. The poignancy of her fate lies in her doomed struggle to subdue that part of her own nature which is no better than her culture. Where a less pliant imagination than Mrs. Wharton's would surely have conceived Lily's conflict with her world as the battle between Innocence (Lily) and Experience (Society), Mrs. Wharton has the courage to recognize the extent to which Lily has herself been tainted by her environment.

One of the subtler themes of *The House of Mirth* is the parallel Mrs. Wharton traces between Lily's defeat and the inevitable defeat of art in a crass materialistic culture. It is not only that Lily herself possesses the quality of a fine work of art, though it is in fact just this that attracts Rosedale to her so that we can conjecture that if

he applies as good taste to the pictures he will soon buy, his collection will be a notable one; it is also that Lily's own ambitions are
those of art. For Mrs. Wharton's heroine, wealth is much more than
a matter of worldly security—and this despite her luxurious tastes
whose indulgence plays such a large part in her undoing. It is the
means for living a life of harmony and grace, free of the dingy and
sordid: Mrs. Wharton repeatedly uses these two words to describe
an existence where there is insufficient money to enhance one's own
potentialities or to disguise the less lovely aspects of life. That the
same small segment of society which is lucky enough to have the
means for making life into a thing of beauty should be as lacking in
virtue and generosity, as lacking, actually, in the instinct to art, as
Lily's friends are is a major irony of her story. With the considerable
bitterness of her intimate experience of the spiritual desolation of
Society, Mrs. Wharton assures us that the rich are morally unworthy
of the beauty they can afford, that at heart they are all of them of
a piece with Mrs. Peniston, whose expensive dismal furniture is
so accurate a reflection of her charmlessness and such an offense to
her niece. Whatever one's wealth, one cannot buy spiritual grace;
nor, by extension, can art redeem a callous humanity. In an extraordinary scene, in which some newcomers to Society herald their
arrival with a lavish party, the climax of which is a series of *tableaux
vivants* reproducing old masterpieces of painting—Goya, Titian,
Veronese, Watteau—Mrs. Wharton puts Lily in the scant draperies
of Reynolds' Mrs. Lloyd and she comments: "It was as though she
had stepped, not out of, but into Reynolds's canvas, banishing
the phantom of his dead beauty by the beams of her living grace."
To Lawrence Selden, Lily's male counterpart in delicacy and
imaginativeness, the apparition catches "for a moment a note of that
eternal harmony of which her beauty was a part," but for Ned
Alstyne, spokesman for a decadent patriciate, Lily's appearance is
the occasion for the only connoisseurship of which his culture is
capable: "Deuced bold thing to show herself in that get-up; but, gad,
there isn't a break in the lines anywhere, and I suppose she wanted
us to know it!" Instead of the self-confirming and ungenerous in her
spectators being outweighed by an experience of the lovely and
eternal, the balance has gone the other way. Lily's "predominance of

personality" (as Mrs. Wharton phrases it) can speak only to what is small-minded in her audience.

Lily's sensibility, her quick eager responsiveness to beauty, has nowhere to exercise itself except in this rich vulgar world to which she has been born. Even Nature, always present where there is the money to buy it, turns out to be only another propitious setting for the advancement of her marital ambitions rather than the ambience for finer feelings than are readily accommodated in dining salons and grand ballrooms; in an encounter with Selden, on a country walk, the tender spell that is put upon the two of them by the glimmer and fragrance of the Hudson Valley landscape is drastically interrupted by Lily's recollection that she must not be missing from the house when the Gryce heir, her current "opportunity," returns to it. As for religion, which in an earlier culture would have been the most promising source of compensation for Lily's deprivations of spiritual sustenance, it has as completely ceased to exist for a person of her imaginativeness as for her crass companions. Young Gryce does indeed go to church, but it is made clear to us that his ritual obedience to the maternal injunction is not to be separated from his cautiousness against chills and tobacco. In this world, piety is a comic attribute and true devoutness unthinkable; there is but one God, Mammon. *The House of Mirth* is always and passionately a money story. It is money that rules where God, love, charity or even force of character or distinction of personality might once have ruled. It is money that puts the wrong persons in power and that robs Lily of the ability to fulfill her potentialities which are so much larger than theirs. It is money that, in killing a Lily Bart, announces its miserable triumph over the human spirit.

Because Lily Bart's story is so much a money story and Lily is herself so consistently at the mercy of her economic disadvantage, one might expect Mrs. Wharton to pass some measure of adverse judgment upon her heroine's failure of sympathy for a class even less privileged than her own. For instance, in Lily's rare excursion into philanthropy the emotions she displays can scarcely be counted to her credit: Selden's cousin, Gerty Farish, is a young woman who has accepted both poverty and spinsterhood in order to pursue a life of good works, and when Lily visits the working-girls' club which is Gerty's particular vocation, she is all gracious condescen-

sion; like a queen among her subjects, she allows the girls to look
upon her beauty so that their own drab lives may be irradiated.
But although vis-à-vis Gerty's deep-rooted devotion to her girls
Lily's shallow pleasure in her ability to bring enchantment into a
dark corner of life is not calculated to endear her to us, long
before this episode, at the very start of the novel, the difference
between Gerty and Lily has been precisely drawn in Lily's favor.
Selden and Lily have been speaking of his cousin, and Lily, having
alluded to the terms of Gerty's life—besides being unmarriageable,
Gerty has "a horrid little place, and no maid, and such queer things
to eat. Her cook does the washing and the food tastes of soap"—
sums up the matter: "We're so different, you know: she likes being
good, and I like being happy." As between a life of dingy virtue
and a life of charm and happiness, or at least the intent of happiness, there is no question of how the artist in Mrs. Wharton responds. Nor is the option for grace a mitigation of her morality.
Happiness is the moral option, the sole moral option available to
a person of sensibility like Lily and her author, and, indeed, the
choice is echoed in the response of all the sympathetic characters
in the story. At the end of the novel, when Lily is ill and desperate,
she accidentally runs into Nettie, one of the girls she had smiled
upon so enchantingly at Gerty's club, and we learn from the girl's
own lips the mysterious uplifting effect Lily's presence had had
upon her in a moment of despair. Lily's personal sweetness and
the illumination of a spirit which attaches itself to the quest for
beauty may have been lost upon the people of established power.
But they have never finally failed to communicate themselves to
Nettie, to Gerty Farish, to Selden, even to Simon Rosedale—to all
the persons in the book who themselves still seek and grow.

Among these few humans in Mrs. Wharton's novel none is more
congenial than Lawrence Selden, the bachelor lawyer who comes to
be Lily's conscience as well as her love. While it no doubt stretches
things to see in Selden a conscious portrait of Henry James, the
connection is perhaps more intimate than Mrs. Wharton could comfortably recognize. True, Selden is a bachelor, not a celibate; he has
had an affair with the promiscuous Mrs. Dorset and we are allowed
to surmise an extended series of sexual alliances that have similarly
left him free of significant emotional entanglement. This sexual

disparity aside, together with the fact that Selden shows no impulse to expatriation, there is nevertheless much to remind us of James in Selden's moral elevation and in the inviolability with which he inhabits an insensible world, as well as in his eager appreciation of beauty and his subtle wit. The intellectual of *The House of Mirth* and, in his quality of spirit, as much an "artist" as Lily, Selden, with his decent bachelor quarters, his good worn rugs and books and his excellent modest teas, is as close to a bohemian as Mrs. Wharton could manage. He cogently argues the thesis that is everywhere implied in Mrs. Wharton's novel, and made explicit in her own choice of a manner of life, that mind and grace of spirit reach their best flower in a well-ordered society, sheltered against the rude winds that blow through a more open world.

Selden is unmarried not because of any insufficient wish for final commitment to a woman. The fact that he is a man of strong passions, if we had ever doubted it, is unmistakable in his response to Lily's appearance in the *tableau vivant*. It is by no accident that Mrs. Wharton has cast Lily in a painting of Reynolds, with whose treatise on the Grand Style she was bound to be familiar. While the idiom of her period imposes the expectable restraints on sexual expression, her description of Lily's beauty of body revealed through thin classical draperies carries a remarkable erotic charge, and we come to perceive, through Mrs. Wharton's manifest pleasure in Lily's pagan sensuality and the approval his author gives to Selden for his warm reception of the scene, that in obeying the injunction of her period against sexual overtness in her fiction Mrs. Wharton is in no way blinding herself to sexual reality. On the contrary, she suggests a radical connection between sensuality and elegance, between sexuality and sensibility. If the well-ordered, the harmonious, and the classical announces itself in grace and highmindedness, Mrs. Wharton concludes that it is also the style that best serves our biological needs. Lily and Selden are designed for each other not merely in spirit but in body.

But Selden cannot take what he wants and should have, and this is almost as much the tragedy of *The House of Mirth* as Lily Bart's social victimization. His passions are strong but blocked—or so we would put it today; they are unavailable to him except as a kind of promissory note on a beneficence to which he lacks access.

Throughout the story, Selden moves toward Lily from behind a
cruel shield of emotional self-protection, always afraid to give over
to the commanding impulse, always defended against the very involvement he could most wish for himself. Incapable of the spontaneous gift of his love, of the instinctual acceptance which would
restore Lily's faith in herself, he manages only to reinforce her
crippling scruples without ever proposing a feasible alternative to
a life which uniquely punishes the weakly conscientious.

Regarding Lily as an unengaged instance of beauty, Selden can be
fundamentally untroubled, and even charmed, by her follies and
trivialities. He is far too genuinely sophisticated to require that art
be validated by solemnity. But so soon as he would make her the
object of emotions that might shake his own tidy system of feelings
or threaten his isolate pride, his first and victorious impulse is
retreat. There is the one occasion, of course, when Lily herself must
take responsibility for his quick defensiveness—when Selden has
made his first groping offer of love and Lily interrupts him to dash
home to Gryce. Although at this point in the novel the reader
is already aware that Lily's conduct is not quite so grim as it looks
and that she just cannot believe that the "real" world of sound
marriages and even sounder bank accounts has room in it for the
happiness she experiences in Selden's company, there is no reason
for Selden himself to take her flight as anything except a gross rejection. But the story goes on and provides Selden, too, with sufficient opportunity to learn what we have always known of Lily, that
she is his for the firm asking, or taking. He nevertheless continues
aloof and suspicious, and eventually he deserts her quite as conspicuously as her other old friends do; the censorious judgment of
the world serves the unconsciously welcome function of protecting
him against his desires. Only when Lily is vindicated in and by
death—on her desk is her check to Trenor in full payment of the
money Trenor had advanced her!—can the emotions that have been
locked in Selden be released. Society turns out, that is, to be the
counterpart, perhaps the sum, of the prohibitions that have always
paralyzed his feelings. It is finally as triumphant over Selden as
over Lily Bart. In yielding to the social authority, Selden has denied
life itself, his own no less than Lily's.

With Lily dead, the light goes out in the world for Selden and of course a little for ourselves too; fiction has presented us with another of its all-too-convincing demonstrations of the toll society exacts in defeated feeling. In a novel contrived like a poem, never a line but has been framed for its precise use in the tragic pattern of the story, never an excessive or ill-considered phrase, we particularly come to notice Mrs. Wharton's reiteration of words that, on the one hand, suggest light—*glow, glimmer, radiance, illumination, sun, shimmer*—and, on the other, evoke darkness—*shadow, dim, dingy, dreary, dull.* Except for *Othello,* or perhaps *Romeo and Juliet,* one can think of no other work of the literary imagination which makes this much verbal play between the images of night and day.

"Dramatize, dramatize!" James exhorted himself, and whether in emulation of the master or because of her own commitment to the formal structure of the novel, Mrs. Wharton sees to it that her story proceeds by *happenings.* In *The House of Mirth,* however, the most crucial happenings turn out to be scarcely more than accidents, or even coincidences. From the start of the book, in which Lily, whiling away time before she takes a train at Grand Central Station, drops in at Selden's bachelor quarters for an innocent cup of tea and is seen not merely by Rosedale, who turns out to own the building, but also by a charwoman who will later abstract Mrs. Dorset's love letters from Selden's trashbasket and offer them to Lily for blackmail purposes, the poor girl can seem to take no step that is not witnessed by the persons who will put it to worst use—to the point where we feel of the Furies who pursue her that they are really only small-town gossips with nothing better to do than lay nasty little traps for their victim and then sit by to watch her fall into them. But then we realize that this is the nature of Mrs. Wharton's, and Lily's, society; their New York is very much a small town where everyone knows everyone else and where the boundaries even upon one's physical movements are rigidly prescribed. Mrs. Peniston, after all, can sit at her window and be as well-informed of the comings and goings of her acquaintances as if she were still young and active. If, in the novel as we know it today, the malign power of society announces itself in our sense of anonymity and of our being overwhelmed by the vast and remote, for Lily Bart it lies in her relentless coercion by the familiar—in her inability to evade the eyes of her world and lose herself in the crowd.

And yet the restrictions of class which are so binding on Lily do not rob her story of wider reference, even to ourselves who are removed from her by such radical social change. Her station in life serves the classic device of presenting us with a common human tragedy in a situation where, because the stakes are unusually high and the fall from glory very steep, the personal defeat has a special poignancy. In much the same way that, without in the least blinding ourselves to the inequities, absurdities and even horrors of Lily Bart's world, we can envy a society as neatly encompassable as this, we can also ignore the incongruities between Lily's situation and ours to discover our own tragic fate in her story. A class novel if ever there was one, *The House of Mirth* wholly transcends the limited social environment with which it is immediately concerned, and perhaps the more successfully because Mrs. Wharton has such a definite social axis around which she organizes her moral perceptions.

On the other hand, few novels of our century or even of a more distant time are as archaic as *The House of Mirth* as a record of the conventions. In Lily's entire dependence on the good opinion of her small segment of society, her naked vulnerability to gossip, her incapacity to make a life for herself or even to stay physically alive except within this restricted world and on its strict terms, we have the data of a way of life, particularly of female life, that is bound to confound the modern reader. Today, when we are more alert than we ever have been to the economic determination of whatever kind of power, we have no trouble understanding that social privilege must be paid for in hard cash. This is very different, however, from inhabiting a society where the right even to earn a living is a social privilege and where ostracism from the class of one's birth is the equivalent of a death sentence.

Early in the novel Lily talks with Selden about poverty; the unreality of her approach to the unhappy subject is revealed in her jesting remark that she has no fear of being poor because she knows how to trim her own hats. It is as unimaginable to her that she will ever have to support herself as that a woman of her class should travel without a maid, so that when, all incredibly, such a moment arrives and she discovers that her aptitude in millinery is something less than a professional talent, she receives the blow with considerable dryness: never having seriously supposed she could move out of her class nor recognized even a human connection with the working class, the failure to qualify for it is not a humiliation; it is just another fatality, another link in the chain of error that has led her to her present plight. Nor is the reader surprised that Mrs. Wharton cannot contrive a more suitable form of employment for Lily—as, say, a governess or companion. Where, as for Lily Bart, society poses but a single alternative to a woman, to live by its laws or die by its laws, any ingenuity that would wish to triumph over the preordained destiny is at best merely a delaying tactic. Like the old Bolshevik who confesses to uncommitted crimes in attestation of the superior moral authority of the state, Lily affirms the absolute power of society over the life of the individual by her demonstration that she is finally incapable of effective action on her own behalf.

The double moral standard, one for the married woman and another for the unmarried, that supports this authoritarian social structure is not an unfamiliar one; we know it from traditional European societies in which a very wide moral latitude is permitted a married woman so long as she has the protection of her husband's name and bank account but where the woman who has not yet reached this economic sanctuary must guard against the slightest misstep. We readily recognize the old economic motive at work in the fact that the very people who are most fierce in condemnation of Lily because she visits Selden or Trenor in compromising circumstances, or because she takes money from the husband of her best friend, can accept unruffled Mrs. Dorset's extramarital excursions or Mrs. Fisher's "loans" from the gentlemen of her acquaintance. But the petty vindictiveness which Mrs. Wharton's matrons direct upon Lily Bart suggests a qualitative difference between the conduct of upper-class Europeans and upper-class Americans in analagous situations of social dissidence. There is little of the high-mindedness of an established aristocracy but much of the spitefulness of the petty bourgeoisie in Mrs. Dorset's retaliations against Lily or in the speed with which all the women of her circle run to cover once Lily falls out of favor with its leaders. And Trenor's easy talk about his benefactions to Lily and the righteous indifference with which he meets the ruin of her reputation scarcely describe a gentleman. It necessarily occurs to us that only a class that has never been certain of its stability or distinction could be this meanly self-protective, and that Mrs. Wharton's decision to ally herself with this section of society was bound, finally, to bring her as much suffering as satisfaction.

The bitterness of *The House of Mirth,* beneath its well-bred surface, is indeed extreme. One has the sense that Mrs. Wharton concentrated in the story of Lily Bart the accumulated angers of her lifetime up to that point—and there would be, we know, still more bitterness to come, and still more novels in which to tell it out. That Mrs. Wharton was able to discipline herself as rigorously as she did, so that the force of her personal feelings never violated her cool imagination of what the novel should be, does great credit to her character. But no doubt it does much to explain the distance at which she has been kept by the modern public.

A Reading of *The House of Mirth*

by *Irving Howe*

I

The House of Mirth begins in a manner characteristic of Mrs. Wharton, with a forthright attack on her material, hard and direct, and without expository preparation. The elaborate hovering over the imagined scene so habitual to Henry James . . . is not at all her way of doing things, for she is a blunt and often impatient writer. "My last page," she once said, "is always latent in my first," and at least in *The House of Mirth* the claim is true. At the very outset Mrs. Wharton groups the main figures of her story—Lily Bart, Lawrence Selden, Sim Rosedale—in several vignettes of typical conduct. These comprise not so much a full novelistic scene as a succession of compressed, scenic fragments, each juxtaposed so as to yield quick information and stir immediate concern. "The art of rendering life in fiction," Mrs. Wharton wrote, "can never . . . be anything . . . but the disengaging of crucial moments from the welter of experience."

That is precisely what she does in the opening chapters. Lily is first seen through the eyes of Selden, the cultivated lawyer who is to serve as a standard of moral refinement and an instance of personal inadequacy. "Her discretions," writes Mrs. Wharton in one of those bristling sentences that do their necessary damage to both Lily and Selden, "interested him almost as much as her imprudences: he was so sure that both were part of the same carefully-elaborated plan." Shrewd yet not sufficiently daring, Selden here begins to

enact that rhythm of involvement and withdrawal, advance and
retreat, which will mark his relations with Lily until the very end
of the book. He entices her with a vision of a life better than the
one she has chosen, yet fails to give her the unquestioning masculine
support which might enable her to live by that vision.

We see Lily and Selden together, each a little uneasy with the
other, yet decidedly attractive as a pair and civilized enough to
take pleasure in knowing they are attractive—Mrs. Wharton had a
fine eye for the pictorial arrangements in the social intercourse
between the sexes. They amuse and test each other with small talk
—Mrs. Wharton had a fine ear for the conversation that carries subtle burdens of meaning. We see Lily and Selden taking each other's
measure, Lily admiring his quiet style yet aware of his handicaps
and hesitations, Selden admiring her beauty yet aware that "she was
so evidently the victim of the civilization which had produced her,
that the links of her bracelet seemed like manacles chaining her to
her fate." This striking sentence is put to several uses: it prepares
us for the ordeal of a Lily Bart neither at ease with nor in rebellion
against her life as a dependent of the rich; it provides a convincing
example of Selden's gift for superior observation; and because, ironically, this gift is matched with his tendency to self-protection and
self-justification, it suggests that Mrs. Wharton will not require nor
allow Selden to serve as a voice of final judgment in the novel.
Given the caustic style of these opening pages, we are entitled to
suppose that Mrs. Wharton will reserve that task for herself.

There quickly follows the encounter between Lily and Rosedale.
At this point Rosedale is mostly stock caricature, the "pushy little
Jew" taken from the imagery of social, that is, polite, anti-Semitism;
later Mrs. Wharton will do more with him. Rosedale trips Lily in a
lie and is not gentleman enough to refrain from stressing his petty
triumph, but the main point is that Lily, usually so nimble at
handling social difficulties, has been caught off balance because
she is still glowing with the pleasure of having met Selden. This too
prefigures a major theme: the price, here in embarrassment and
later in deprivation, that genuine emotion exacts from those who
have chosen a life of steady calculation. Coming always at inconvenient moments—for it is Selden's presence which repeatedly causes

her to falter—the spontaneous feelings Lily neither can nor wishes to suppress will lead to her social undoing.

Lovely as Lily Bart seems, Mrs. Wharton is careful to establish a firm dissociation between author and heroine, though never to the point of withdrawing her compassion. The similarity between Rosedale and Lily, each trying in a particular way to secure a foothold in the world of the rich, is faintly suggested by Mrs. Wharton as a cue for later elaboration. She also introduces the figure of Lily's cousin, Jack Stepney, who serves as Lily's Smerdyakov, the "double" grossly reflecting and disfiguring her ambitions. Lily, as Mrs. Wharton dryly remarks, "understood his motives, for her own course was guided by as nice calculations."

And then, to climax these introductory chapters, there come two moments of symbolic action, each isolating the central role of money in the life of Lily Bart. The first is Balzacian: Judy Trenor, the rich hostess and for a time Lily's friend, "who could have afforded to lose a thousand a night [at cards], had left the table clutching such a heap of bills that she had been unable to shake hands with her guests when they bade her good night." The second is probably beyond Balzac: Lily, having lost too much money at cards, retires to her room in the Trenor house and notices "two little lines near her mouth, faint flaws in the smooth curve of her cheek." Frightened, she thinks they may be caused by the electric light. She turns it off, leaving only the candles on her dressing-table. "The white oval of her face swam out waveringly from a background of shadows, the uncertain light blurring it like a haze; but the two lines about the mouth remained."

. . . At every point Lily's history is defined by her journey from one social group to another, a journey both she and her friends regard as a fall, a catastrophe. Only dimly, and then after much pain and confusion, does she realize that this social fall may have positive moral consequences. For us, who have followed her story with that mixture of ironic detachment and helpless compassion Mrs. Wharton trains us to feel, it should be clear all the while that the meanings of the book emerge through a series of contrasts between a fixed scale of social place and an evolving measure of moral value.

It is as if the world within which Lily moves consists of a series of descending planes, somewhat like a modern stage, and each part of the novel is devoted to showing the apparent success with which Lily survives one drop after another but also how each apparent success bears within itself the impetus toward still another fall. As Mrs. Wharton remarks: "If [Lily] slipped she recovered her footing, and it was only afterward that she was aware of having recovered it each time on a slightly lower level." There is, to be sure, much more to *The House of Mirth* than these expert notations of social status. There is a portrait of a young woman trapped in her confusions of value, a story of love destroyed through these confusions, and a harsh enactment of Mrs. Wharton's sentiments about human loss and doom. But all of these take on their particular cogency, their fictional shape, under the pressures of the social milieu evoked in the novel.

Mrs. Wharton's great theme—the dispossession of the old New York aristocracy by the vulgar new rich—is not quite so visible in, *The House of Mirth* as in *The Custom of the Country* or *The Age of Innocence*. The action of *The House of Mirth* occurs in the first years of the twentieth century, several stages and a few decades beyond the dispossession of old New York. We barely see any representatives of the faded aristocracy; what we do see in the first half of the book are several of its distant offshoots and descendants, most of them already tainted by the vulgarity of the new bourgeoisie yet, for no very good reasons, still contemptuous of it. The standards of those characters who have any claim to the old aristocracy are not so much guides to their own conduct as strategies for the exclusion of outsiders. Like Gus Trenor, they have kept some pretense to social superiority but very little right to it, and even an exceptional figure like Lawrence Selden, who does try to live by cultivated standards, has been forced into a genteel bohemianism and an acceptance of his failure to act with manly decisiveness.

In no way is the old aristocracy, or even the *idea* of the old aristocracy, held up as a significant model for behavior. Indeed, in *The House of Mirth* the moral positives seem almost disembodied, hovering like ghosts over the figures of Lily Bart and Lawrence Selden. When the new rich make their assault upon the world of the established rich, there occurs a brief contest between an aspiring and an entrenched snobbism, and soon enough, as one might expect, a truce is struck. The victim of that truce is Lily Bart.

Each step in Lily's decline allows Mrs. Wharton to examine the moral ugliness of still another segment of the wealthy classes. In the novel Lily begins with

> *The Trenors,* who maintain a pretense of loyalty to traditional styles and values, even while frequently violating them. That they feel obliged to keep up this pretense does, however, have a restraining influence upon their conduct. Gus Trenor may harass Lily, but she can still appeal successfully to his sense of being a gentleman ("old habits . . . the hand of inherited order . . ."). Once dropped by the Trenors—a major sign she is slipping—Lily finds a place with

> *The Dorsets,* who are at least as rich and socially powerful as the Trenors but in Mrs. Wharton's hierarchy occupy a lower rung. They no longer pretend to care about traditional styles and values. Bertha Dorset is a ferocious bitch, her husband a limp dyspeptic. They ruthlessly abandon Lily and she, no longer able to stay afloat in her familiar element, must now turn to the new rich. She does this with the help of

> *Carrie Fisher,* a brilliantly portrayed figure who acts as guide for those *arrivistes* willing to pay for their social acceptance. Frankly materialistic, yet likable for her candor, Mrs. Fisher is troubled neither by Lily's scruples nor her delusions, and for a time she arranges that Lily find refuge with

> *The Brys,* very rich and feverishly on the make. Gus Trenor may sneer when the Brys give their expensive "crush," but he goes and thereby helps to seal the fusion between his set and all that the Brys represent. Unable or unwilling to remain with the Brys, Lily finds a haven of sorts with

> *The Gormers,* who also have large amounts of money but care less for status than pleasure. Once, however, Mrs. Gormer is tempted socially by the poisonous Bertha Dorset, Lily finds herself displaced again and must take refuge with

> *Norma Hatch,* the wealthy divorcee who lives in a chaos of indolence, forever a prey to sharpers and schemers. Lily finds this atmosphere intolerable, and nothing remains for her but the last fall into the abyss of poverty.

As Lily goes down step by step, two figures stand on the sidelines observing her and occasionally troubling to intervene, but never decisively, never with full heart or unqualified generosity. Selden feels an acute sympathy for her, but a sympathy marred by fastidiousness; he loves her, but except for the last moment, not with a love prepared to accept the full measure of its risks. Rosedale sees her as a possible asset for his social climb and later finds himself vaguely moved by her troubles, but at the end he turns away, convinced she has lost her market value. Selden's ethical perceptions are as superior to Lily's as Rosedale's are inferior, but Mrs. Wharton, with her corrosive and thrusting irony, places the two men in a relationship of symmetrical exposure. In Mrs. Wharton's world men are often weak, either too refined for action or too coarse for understanding: they fail one, they do not come through. . . . Lily ends her days alone.

II

The social setting of *The House of Mirth* is elaborated with complete assurance: one is always persuaded of the tangibility of Mrs. Wharton's milieu, the precision with which she observes nuances of status and place. But what finally draws and involves us is the personal drama enacted within this setting. Lily Bart is a victim of taste, both good and bad: she has a natural taste for moral and esthetic refinements which causes her to be repelled by the world of the rich, and she has an acquired taste for luxury that can be satisfied only in that world. She is too fine in her perceptions to act ruthlessly enough to achieve her worldly aims, and too much the captive of those aims to be able to live by her perceptions. She has enough moral awareness to respect civilized structures of behavior, but not enough moral courage to abandon the environment in which they are violated. She is trapped in a heart struggle between the pleasures of this world, that is, to lure the dismal millionaire Gryce into marriage, and the refinements of personal relations, which means to drop Gryce for the privilege of walking with Lawrence Selden on a Sunday afternoon. She pays, in the words of Percy Lubbock, "for her fastidiousness by finding herself abandoned by the vivid crowd: and she pays for her courtship of the crowd, so carefully taught her by all the conditions of life, by discovering that

her independence is only strong enough to destroy and not to remake her life."

Simply as an example of imaginative portraiture, Lily Bart is
one of the triumphs of American writing. Mrs. Wharton has succeeded in that supremely difficult task of the novelist: to show a
figure in plasticity and vibration while preserving the firm outlines
of her conception. We soon grasp the nature of Lily's character, yet
are repeatedly surprised and moved by its local shadings. Mrs.
Wharton does not for a moment soften the judgments that Lily
invites, nor does she hesitate to expose all of Lily's weakness and
self-indulgence. Lily "was fond of pictures and flowers, and of
sentimental fiction, and she could not help thinking that the possession of such tastes ennobled her desire for worldly advantage."
And a still more biting sentence: "Selden's reputed civilization was
generally regarded as a slight obstacle to easy intercourse, but Lily,
who prided herself on her broad-minded recognition of literature,
and always carried an Omar Khayam in her traveling-bag, was attracted by this attribute, which she felt would have had its distinction in an older society." Through a steady accumulation of
incidents Mrs. Wharton makes it clear that Lily is pitifully lacking
in any core of personal being. At home neither in the Trenor mansion nor Selden's book-lined rooms nor the shabby apartment of
her cousin Gerty Farish, Lily is at the mercy of her restlessness, a
strangely disabling kind of restlessness which marks an unfinished
self. Yet all of these judgments are stated or implied by Mrs. Wharton with a profound compassion, a sense of the sadness that comes
to one in observing a lovely human being dash herself against the
rocks of her own bewilderment. If Lily cannot maintain those flashes
of self-awareness that come to her in moments of failure, she is still
a generous and warm-hearted woman, open, in Mrs. Wharton's
magnificent phrase, to "one of those sudden shocks of pity that
sometimes decentralize a life."

Lily's fall is treated partly as a naturalistic drama in which a
victim of circumstance is slowly crushed. She admires Selden because

he had preserved . . . a happy air of viewing the show objectively,
of having points of contact outside the great gilt cage. . . . How

alluring the world outside the cage appeared to Lily, as she heard its door clang on her! In reality, as she knew, the door never clanged: it stood always open; but most of the captives were like flies in a bottle, and having once flown in, could never regain their freedom.

This sense of fatality in *The House of Mirth* is reinforced, step by step, as Lily confronts the social demarcations of her world. . . . The ordeal of Lily Bart continues to be a significant one, even if its terms and setting have come to seem historically dated. In one way or another, the problem of mediating between the expectations of a commercial society and the ideals of humane civilization is not exactly unknown to us; only on the surface is our society so very different from that of Lily Bart.

This view of the novel is not accepted, however, by certain critics who question whether Lily's fate is very important or deeply affecting, and who see in her story little more than the malaise of an idle woman unable to dispense with privileges. In a phrase of dismissal Henry Seidel Canby has written of *The House of Mirth* that "it reveals nothing in the history of Lily Bart which wealth would not cure." He is wrong; exactly the opposite is true. Mrs. Wharton goes to some pains to stress that wealth lies within Lily's grasp if only she will do what she cannot bring herself to do: make sacrifices of taste, forgo assumptions of honor, accept conditions of tedium. That Lily yearns for wealth is obvious; that anyone could suppose it to be a "cure" for her is astonishing. But apart from his inaccuracy, Mr. Canby's statement displays a somewhat comic complacence: he writes as if the pressures of financial need had nothing to do with human suffering in our time, as if true tragedy were something apart from the hustle of daily life, and as if literary critics never worked themselves into a moral corner through a conflict between desires and standards. Lily Bart, to be sure, is not a heroine in the grand style: she is a weak and lovely woman. Her life, torn apart by what Mrs. Wharton calls "the eternal struggle between man's contending impulses," may not satisfy the Aristotelian concept of tragedy. But to say this is perhaps nothing more than to suggest how limited a value there is in applying such concepts to modern literature.

In any case, our response to Lily can hardly be exhausted by the sum of moral judgments we make about her. Once all statements of discount have been entered against Lily, we remain concerned and stirred by her effort—who has not known or experienced similar ones?—to bring together irreconcilable ways of life. Before the pathos of her failure, judgment fades into love.

III

The House of Mirth is not written in the kind of prose, favored in many twentieth century novels, that aims to resemble a transparent glass, a clear window upon the action. Mrs. Wharton's prose solicits attention in its own right. It asks us constantly to be aware of an authorial voice speaking with a full readiness to provide comment and generalization. At various points in the novel we are allowed some entrance into Lily Bart's mind, but never to the point of forgetting that it is Mrs. Wharton who guides us there and will soon be guiding us away. We are always conscious that the narrative comes to us through a style of high polish, austere irony, epigrammatic conciseness. What Mrs. Wharton says in her own right is just as much a part of the texture of the novel as the action and the dialogue.

Her style impresses one by its capacity for severe qualifications. Here is Mrs. Wharton on Bertha Dorset:

> She was smaller and thinner than Lily Bart, with a restless pliability of pose, as if she could have been crumpled up and run through a ring, like the sinuous draperies she affected. Her small pale face seemed the mere setting of a pair of dark exaggerated eyes, of which the visionary gaze contrasted curiously with her self-assertive tone and gestures; so that, as one of her friends observed, she was like a disembodied spirit who took up a great deal of room.

The writing here is extremely vivid, partly as a visual description of Bertha Dorset, but primarily as a generalized evocation of Mrs. Wharton's sense and judgment of her. There are numerous other examples that might be given for this power of concise and neat generalization. One remembers, as a comic instance, the sentence about Lily's dreary aunt: "Mrs. Peniston thought the country lonely

and trees damp, and cherished a vague fear of meeting a bull." Or
an instance of Mrs. Wharton's gift for dramatic summation: "It was
success that dazzled [Lily]—she could distinguish facts plainly
enough in the twilight of failure." Or Mrs. Wharton's capacity for
a kind of statement that pertains both to the matter in hand and
larger issues of human experience: Gerty Farish, pleased that Lily
has contributed to a charity, "supposed her beautiful friend to be
actuated by the same motive as herself—that sharpening of the
moral vision which makes all human suffering so near and insistent
that the other aspects of life fade into remoteness."

But even as one comes to savor the crispness of Mrs. Wharton's
prose, there are passages in *The House of Mirth* that leave one
uneasy. Usually these are passages in which she reveals the unfortunate tendency toward ladies'-magazine rhetoric that broke out in
her later years. And usually they are passages in which she must
confront a theme—the satisfactions of romantic love—she finds
either too embarrassing or too upsetting to handle with ease. Writing about an encounter between Selden and Lily, she composes a
sentence that, at least in its second clause, seems decidedly forced:
"it was one of those moments when neither seemed to speak deliberately, when an indwelling voice in each called to the other
across unsounded depths of feeling." Here is Mrs. Wharton's description of the last talk between Selden and Lily, utterly right
in its first sentence and a purple lapse in the second:

> Something in truth lay dead between them—the love she had killed
> in him and could no longer call to life. But something lived between
> them also, and leaped up in her like an imperishable flame: it was the
> love his love had kindled, the passion of her soul for his.

To notice this stylistic problem is to approach a central limitation
of Mrs. Wharton's writing. . . . Her work overwhelms us with its
harsh truths, but finally it seems incomplete and earth-bound. Mrs.
Wharton believed firmly in the moral positives she had inherited,
but she could seldom project them into her work; all too often they
survive only in terms of their violation. Hence the grinding, un-
relenting, impatient tone of her work as if she sensed some deficiency,
perhaps in the very scheme of things or only in her own vision,

and did not know how to fill the need. Mrs. Wharton was a thoroughly conservative writer but there are times one is inclined to say, a bit paradoxically, that she is too hard on the rich, too glacial in her contempt for their mediocrity, too willing to slash away at them because she does not know anyone else to turn toward or against.

Such difficulties occur to one mainly in retrospect. When one reads and submits to the urgencies of a novel like *The House of Mirth,* the effect is that of being held in a steady, inexorable enclosure. Mrs. Wharton's sense of the inescapability of waste—the waste of spirit, the waste of energy, the waste of beauty—comes to seem a root condition of human life. In her autobiography she wrote, "life is the saddest thing there is, next to death," and the best of her novels force us to entertain the possibility she is right.

On *Ethan Frome*

by Blake Nevius

. . . Although much has been made of this minor classic of our literature as a picture of New England life and a triumph of style and construction, its relation to Mrs. Wharton's more characteristic and important stories has never been clearly established. *Ethan Frome* is not a "sport." It belongs to the main tradition of Mrs. Wharton's fiction, and it has a value, independent of its subject and technique, in helping us to define that tradition. Alfred Kazin has linked it to *The House of Mirth* as a demonstration of the spiritual value of failure, but although this is a recurrent theme in Edith Wharton, particularly in the novels she wrote in the Twenties, and is inescapable in the conclusion of *The House of Mirth*, it is no mean feat, I think, to reconcile it with the episode which forms the narrative framework of *Ethan Frome*. She was by no means convinced of its soundness, and it is possible, as I intend to suggest, that the spectacle of Ethan's prolonged and hopeless defeat, reinforced by the glimpses of his spiritual isolation, his scarred and twisted body, and his querulous, demanding womenfolk, is intended to convey quite the opposite of what Mr. Kazin finds in the story.

The final, lingering note of the story, it seems to me, is one of despair arising from the contemplation of spiritual waste. So emphatic is it that it drowns out the conventional notion of the value of suffering and defeat. Ethan himself sounds it just before his last, abortive effort to escape his destiny:

> Other possibilities had been in him, possibilities sacrificed, one by one, to Zeena's narrow-mindedness and ignorance. And what good had

come of it? She was a hundred times bitterer and more discontented
than when he had married her: the one pleasure left her was to inflict
pain on him. All the healthy instincts of self-defense rose up in him
against such waste. . . .

And taking Mrs. Wharton's novels as a whole, that note swells into
a refrain whose burden, as George Darrow in *The Reef* formulates
it, is "the monstrousness of useless sacrifices." Here is the ultimate
result of that "immersion of the larger in the smaller nature which
is one of the mysteries of the moral life." As a theme, the vanity of
self-sacrifice is merged repeatedly with the primary theme of the
limits of individual responsibility. A realization of "the monstrousness of useless sacrifices" encourages the characters' selfish, passional
bent, which is curbed in turn by the puritanical assertion of responsibility. For Ethan as for most of Edith Wharton's protagonists who
are confronted by the same alternatives—Ann Eliza Bunner, Newland Archer, Charlotte Lovell, Kate Clephane, Nona Manford,
Martin Boyne—the inherited sense of duty is strong enough to con-
quer, but the victory leaves in its wake the sense of futility which
self-sacrifice entails. Their moral transactions are such as to preclude
a satisfactory balancing of accounts.

How and to what degree does the situation in *Ethan Frome* embody this conflict? No element in the characterization of Ethan is
more carefully brought out than the suggestion of his useful, even
heroic possibilities. He had longed to become an engineer, had acquired some technical training, and is still reading desultorily in
the field when the narrator encounters him. This is one aspect of his
personality. There is still another which helps explain why Edith
Wharton, who was deeply drawn to nature, is predisposed to treat
his case with the utmost sympathy: "He had always been more sensitive than people about him to the appeal of natural beauty. His
unfinished studies had given form to this sensibility and even in
his unhappiest moments field and sky spoke to him with a deep and
powerful persuasion." Add to these qualities his superior gifts of
kindness, generosity, and sociability, and his impressive physical
appearance ("Even then he was the most striking figure in Starkfield, though he was but the ruin of a man"), and it is evident that
Edith Wharton set about, as Melville did with Ahab, to invest her
rather unpromising human material with a tragic dignity.

It is in view of his potentialities that Ethan's marriage to Zeena is a catastrophe. By the time Mattie Silver appears on the scene, he is only twenty-eight but already trapped by circumstances and unable to extend the horizon of his future beyond the family graveyard. Mattie, once she has become the victim of Zeena's jealousy, offers a way out which Ethan is quick to follow. But immediately his plans are set afoot, things begin to close in on him again: farm and mill are mortgaged, he has no credit, and time is against him. Moreover, even in the heat of his resentment he cannot disregard Zeen's plight: "It was only by incessant labor and personal supervision that Ethan drew a meager living from the land, and his wife, even if she were in better health than she imagined, could never carry such a burden alone." His rebellion dies out, but only to be rekindled the next morning as Mattie is about to leave. Suddenly it occurs to him that if he pleads Zeena's illness and the need of a servant, Andrew Hale may give him an advance on some lumber. He starts on foot for Starkfield, meets Mrs. Hale en route, is touched by her expression of sympathy ("You've had an awful mean time, Ethan Frome"), continues toward his rendezvous—and is suddenly pulled up short by the realization that he is planning to appeal to the Hales' sympathy to obtain money from them on false pretenses. It is the turning point of the action:

> With the sudden perception of the point to which his madness had carried him, the madness fell and he saw his life before him as it was. He was a poor man, the husband of a sickly woman, whom his desertion would leave alone and destitute; and even if he had the heart to desert her he could have done so only by deceiving two kindly people who had pitied him.

Although he is neatly hemmed in by circumstances, it is Ethan's own sense of responsibility that blocks the last avenue of escape and condemns him to a life of sterile expiation.

In *Ethan Frome* all the themes I have mentioned are developed without the complexity that the more sophisticated characters and setting of *The Fruit of the Tree* and (as we shall see) *The Reef* require; they are reduced to the barest statement of their possibilities. To a person of Ethan's limited experience and his capacity for straightforward judgments, the issues present themselves with the least ambiguity or encouragement to evasion; and in this, I believe, we have the measure of the subject's value for Mrs. Wharton. As her characters approach her own sphere, their motives are disentangled with increasing difficulty from her own, and their actions are regulated by a closer censure; they become more complex and are apt to lose their way amid fine distinctions and tentative judgments. They are aware, like Woburn in the short story "A Cup of Cold Water," of the impossibility of basing a decision upon absolutes:

> Was not all morality based on a convention? What was the stanchest code of ethics but a trunk with a series of false bottoms? Now and then one had the illusion of getting down to absolute right or wrong, but it was only a false bottom—a removable hypothesis—with another false bottom underneath. There was no getting beyond the relative.

Ethan Frome is closer than any of her other characters to the source of the ideas that underlie Edith Wharton's ethical judgments. Puritanism has lost very little of its hold on that portion of the New England mind which he represents and its ideas have not been weakened, as they have in the more populous industrial and commercial centers, by two centuries of enlightenment based on what Bernard Shaw called the Mercanto-Christian doctrine of morality. It is not surprising that many persons unacquainted with Edith Wharton's biography associate her—and not wholly on the strength of *Ethan Frome*—with Boston or with New England as a whole. Whatever the influences exerted by her New York origin and background and her long career abroad, it is the moral order of Ethan Frome's world that governs the view of reality in all her novels.

For this reason, and for others I will suggest, I am unable to appreciate John Crowe Ransom's objections to Mrs. Wharton's handling of point of view in *Ethan Frome,* a problem he assumes to have bothered her more than I suspect it really did. In trying to reconstruct her approach to a solution, he writes that "if Ethan should tell it himself, it would not be identifiable with the main body of Mrs. Wharton's fiction." I am not sure why it is absolutely desirable that it *should* be, but at any rate, the difficulty does not seem to have bothered the author of either *The Bunner Sisters* or *Summer,* which are no more readily identifiable than *Ethan Frome* with her usual subjects. "But if she should tell it," Ransom continues, "it

would very likely be the story of a rather metamorphosed Ethan."
Her "trained and sophisticated sensibility . . . would have falsified
the whole." To this last suggestion, one can only reply that it would
have in any case, whatever point of view she might have chosen.
Nevertheless, Ransom concludes that she "temporized": "She in-
vented a special reporter for Ethan in the person of a young man of
sensibility and education very like her own. In theory it gained
for her this, that the reporter became a man; and this, that not
being herself he need not render quite the complete spiritual history
of events associated with her name as an author. In effect, it gained
her very little."

This is raising difficulties where they do not necessarily exist. In
the first place, Edith Wharton was simply following the structural
method of Balzac's "La Grand Bretèche," as her hint in the preface
and a comparison of the stories will confirm. She did not apply it
with Balzac's success, however, for, as Ransom has correctly noted,
her narrator's "vision" of Ethan's story (not "version," as Ransom
misquotes) is based in large part on data that we cannot imagine
any of the principals supplying, so that the story *is* in reality a
"vision" rather than a "version." In the second place, the narrators
employed in the framework of Edith Wharton's early stories are
always men—whether because she had, as her contemporaries
claimed, a masculine mind or because this refinement of the point of
view allowed her greater freedom, I am not sure. But the choice is
particularly defensible in *Ethan Frome,* first, because the narrator
must have a pretext for visiting Starkfield, and this is more easily
supplied for an engineer than for a woman with the requisite "sensibility and education," and second, because there must be some
probability established for Ethan's inviting the narrator into his
home—over and above, that is, the accident of the storm. Finally,
I am not so willing to assume, as Ransom and many others have,
that ten years' residence in the Berkshires (even allowing for the
annual jaunts to Europe) was not enough to give Mrs. Wharton
the needed understanding of the lives of her poorer neighbors.
"When the mind is imaginative," writes Henry James in *The Art of
Fiction,* ". . . it takes to itself the faintest hints of life, it converts
the very pulses of the air into revelations." In *The Valley of Decision* Edith Wharton had already demonstrated that she could do

this with the materials of history. Why not, then, with the life just beyond her doorstep? . . .

Ethan Frome marks a gain in artistry that was to be consolidated later in *The Reef* and *The Age of Innocence*. The first important work to appear after Edith Wharton had established her permanent residence abroad, it had been undertaken as an exercise in French to modernize her idioms, but had been abandoned after a few weeks. A sojourn at the Mount, some years later, had revived the story in her mind, and it had been written in Paris during the following winter. From the directness and simplicity of the style of the final version, one might suppose that it had been composed entirely in French and then translated, but it was in fact an independent growth from the original seed. She and Walter Berry had "talked the tale over page by page," and the results of their collaboration may be glimpsed in the fragment of a working version preserved among the manuscripts at Yale. Berry was a rigorous taskmaster. "With each book," Edith Wharton acknowledged gratefully, "he exacted a higher standard in economy of expression, in purity of language, in the avoidance of the hackneyed and precious." The stylistic restraint of the final version, unusual even for Mrs. Wharton, may in part be a tribute to his discipline. How many revisions the tale underwent may never be known, but a comparison of the manuscript fragment with the corresponding portion of the printed text indicates that Edith Wharton worked hard to meet Berry's standards and to eliminate redundancies, circumlocutions, and ambiguous or misleading expressions, realizing that the language as well as the theme of *Ethan Frome* had to be treated "starkly and summarily."

Enough has been said, by Mrs. Wharton among others, about the technical resourcefulness brought into play by the peculiar difficulties of telling Ethan's story; but in view of the widespread feeling that the author's human sympathies were hobbled by her rationalism, it should be stressed that the best touches in the story are there because she felt her subject deeply enough to be able to charge it with conviction at every point. The details are few but impressive; they arise directly and easily, and always with the sharpest pertinence, from the significant grounds of character and situation; they are, as Percy Lubbock suggests, "the natural and sufficient channels of great emotion." Every reader will recall some of them: Mattie's tribute to the winter sunset—"It looks just as if it was painted"; Ethan's reluctance to have Mattie see him follow Zeena into their bedroom; the removal of Mattie's trunk; the watchful, sinister presence of Zeena's cat disturbing the intimacy of the lovers' evening together by appropriating her mistress' place at the table, breaking the pickle dish, and later setting Zeena's rocking chair in motion. Zeena may not be a sympathetic character, but there is a moment when she makes us forget everything but her wronged humanity. As she confronts the guilty lovers, holding the fragments of her beloved pickle dish, her face streaming with tears, we have a sudden and terrible glimpse of the starved emotional life that has made her what she is. The novelist's compassion can reach no further.

Although it functioned generally at a mundane level, Edith Wharton's imagination could occasionally be roused to symbol-making activity by the conjunction of a theme and a setting both deeply cherished and understood. In *Ethan Frome* her theme is enhanced by every feature of the landscape: by the "orchard of starved appletrees writhing over a hillside among outcroppings of slate," the crazily slanted headstones in the Frome graveyard, the truncated "L" of Ethan's farmhouse in which one saw "the image of his own shrunken body," but predominantly by the landscape as a whole, buried under snow, silent and incommunicative as the characters. The method looks ahead to *Summer*, with its naturalistic symbol of the Mountain and its subtle accommodation of the human drama to the rhythm of the changing seasons; to the moment in *The Reef* when Darrow recalls his vision of Anna Summers advancing toward him slowly down an avenue of trees, now transformed in his imagination to the passing years, with the "light and shade of old memories and new hopes playing variously on her"; and to *Hudson River Bracketed*, with its dominating symbol of the Willows, equated in Vance Weston's mind with the Past he is struggling to recapture in his first novel. Only in *Ethan Frome*, however, is the symbolism sustained by every element in the setting. It is the one occasion in her longer fiction when her imagination worked freely and without faltering in this extra dimension. . . .

The Morality of Inertia

by *Lionel Trilling*

A theological seminary in New York planned a series of lectures on "The Literary Presentations of Great Moral Issues," and invited me to give one of the talks. Since I have a weakness for the general subject, I was disposed to accept the invitation. But I hesitated over the particular instance, for I was asked to discuss the moral issues in *Ethan Frome*. I had not read Edith Wharton's little novel in a good many years, and I remembered it with no pleasure or admiration. I recalled it as not at all the sort of book that deserved to stand in a list which included *The Brothers Karamazov* and *Billy Budd, Foretopman*. If it presented a moral issue at all, I could not bring to mind what that issue was. And so I postponed my acceptance of the invitation and made it conditional upon my being able to come to terms with the subject assigned to me.

Ethan Frome, when I read it again, turned out to be pretty much as I had recalled it, not a great book or even a fine book, but a factitious book, perhaps even a cruel book. I was puzzled to understand how it ever came to be put on the list, why anyone should want to have it discussed as an example of moral perception. Then I remembered its reputation, which, in America, is very considerable. It is sometimes spoken of as an American classic. It is often assigned to high school and college students as a text for study.

But the high and solemn repute in which it stands is, I am sure, in large part a mere accident of American culture. *Ethan Frome* appeared in 1911, at a time when, to a degree that we can now only wonder at, American literature was committed to optimism, cheerfulness, and gentility. What William Dean Howells called the "smiling aspects of life" had an importance in the literature of America some fifty years ago which is unmatched in the literature of any other time and place. It was inevitable that those who were critical of the prevailing culture and who wished to foster in America higher and more serious literature should put a heavy stress upon the grimmer aspects of life, that they should equate the smiling aspects with falsehood, the grimmer aspects with truth. For these devoted people, sickened as they were by cheerfulness and hope, the word "stark" seemed to carry the highest possible praise a critical review or a blurb could bestow, with "relentless" and "inevitable" as its proper variants. *Ethan Frome* was admired because it was "stark"—its action, we note, takes place in the New England village of Starkville— and because the fate it describes is *relentless* and *inevitable*.

No one would wish to question any high valuation that may be given to the literary representation of unhappy events—except, perhaps, as the high valuation may be a mere cliché of an intellectual class, except as it is supposed to seem the hallmark of the superior sensibility and intelligence of that class. When it is only this, we have the right, and the duty, to look sniffishly at starkness, and relentlessness, and inevitability, to cock a skeptical eye at grimness. And I am quite unable to overcome my belief that *Ethan Frome* enjoys its high reputation because it still satisfies our modern snobbishness about tragedy and pain.

We can never speak of Edith Wharton without some degree of respect. She brought to her novels a strong if limited intelligence, notable powers of observation, and a genuine desire to tell the truth —a desire which in some part she satisfied. But she was a woman in whom we cannot fail to see a limitation of heart, and this limitation makes itself manifest as a literary and moral deficiency of her work, and of *Ethan Frome* especially. It appears in the deadness of her prose, and more flagrantly in the suffering of her characters. Whenever the characters of a story suffer, they do so at the behest of their author—the author is responsible for their suffering and must justify his cruelty by the seriousness of his moral intention. The author of *Ethan Frome*, it seemed to me as I read the book again to test my memory of it, could not lay claim to any such justification. Her intention in writing the story was not adequate to the dreadful fate she contrived for her characters. She indulges herself by what she contrives—she is, as the phrase goes, "merely literary." This is not to say that the merely literary intention does not make its very considerable effects. There is in *Ethan Frome* an image of life-in-death, of hell-on-earth, which is not easily forgotten: the crippled Ethan, and Zeena, his dreadful wife, and Mattie, the once charming girl he had loved, now bedridden and querulous with pain, all living out their death in the kitchen of the desolate Frome farm—a perpetuity of suffering memorializes a moment of passion. It is terrible to contemplate, it is unforgettable, but the mind can do nothing with it, can only endure it.

My new reading of the book, then, did not lead me to suppose that it justified its reputation, but only confirmed my recollection that *Ethan Frome* was a dead book, the product of mere will, of the cold hard literary will. What is more, it seemed to me quite unavailable for any moral discourse. In the context of morality, there is nothing to say about *Ethan Frome*. It presents no moral issue at all. For consider the story it tells. A young man of good and gentle character is the only son of a New England farm couple. He has some intellectual gifts and some desire to know the world, and for a year he is happy attending a technical school. But his father is incapacitated by a farm accident, and Ethan dutifully returns to manage the failing farm and sawmill. His father dies; his mother loses her mental faculties, and during her last illness she is nursed by a female relative whom young Ethan marries, for no other reason than that he is bemused by loneliness. The new wife, Zeena, immediately becomes a shrew, a harridan and a valetudinarian—she lives only to be ill. Because Zeena now must spare herself, the Fromes take into their home a gentle and charming young girl, a destitute cousin of the wife. Ethan and Mattie fall in love, innocently but deeply. The wife, perceiving this, plans to send the girl away, her place to be taken by a servant whose wages the husband cannot possibly afford. In despair at the thought of separation Mattie and Ethan attempt suicide. They mean to die by sledding down a steep hill and crashing into a great elm at the bottom. Their plan fails: both survive the crash, Ethan to be sorely crippled, Mattie to be bedridden in perpetual pain. Now the wife Zeena surrenders her claim to a mysterious pathology and becomes the devoted nurse and jailer of the lovers. The terrible tableau to which I have referred is ready for inspection.

It seemed to me that it was quite impossible to talk about this story. This is not to say that the story is without interest as a story, but what interest it may have does not yield discourse, or at least not moral discourse.

But as I began to explain to the lecture committee why I could not accept the invitation to lecture about the book, it suddenly came over me how very strange a phenomenon the book made— how remarkable it was that a story should place before us the dreadful image of three ruined and tortured lives, showing how their ruin came about, and yet propose no moral issue of any kind. And if *issue* seems to imply something more precisely formulated than we have a right to demand of a story, then it seemed to me no less remarkable that the book had scarcely any moral reverberation, that strange and often beautiful sound we seem to hear generated in the air by a tale of suffering, a sound which is not always music, which does not always have a "meaning," but which yet entrances us, like the random notes of an Aeolian harp, or merely the sound of the wind in the chimney. The moral sound that *Ethan Frome* makes is a dull thud. And this seemed to me so remarkable, indeed, that in the very act of saying why I could not possibly discuss *Ethan Frome*, I found the reason why it must be discussed.

It is, as I have suggested, a very great fault in *Ethan Frome* that it presents no moral issue, sets off no moral reverberation. A certain propriety controls the literary representation of human suffering. This propriety dictates that the representation of pain may not be, as it were, gratuitous; it must not be an end in itself. The naked act of representing, or contemplating, human suffering is a self-indulgence, and it may be a cruelty. Between a tragedy and a spectacle in the Roman circus there is at least this much similarity, that the pleasure both afford derives from observing the pain of others. A tragedy is always on the verge of cruelty. What saves it from the actuality of cruelty is that it has an intention beyond itself. This intention may be so simple a one as that of getting us to do something practical about the cause of the suffering or to help actual sufferers, or at least to feel that we should; or it may lead us to look beyond apparent causes to those which the author wishes us to think of as more real, such as Fate, or the will of the gods, or the will of God; or it may challenge our fortitude or intelligence or piety.

A sense of the necessity of some such intention animates all considerations of the strange paradox of tragedy. Aristotle is concerned to solve the riddle of how the contemplation of human suffering can possibly be pleasurable, of why its pleasure is permissible. He wanted to know what literary conditions were needed to keep a tragedy from being a display of horror. Here it is well to remember that the Greeks were not so concerned as we have been led to believe to keep all dreadful things off the stage—in the presentation of Aristotle's favorite tragedy, the audience saw Jocasta hanging from a beam, it saw the representation of Oedipus' bloody eye-sockets. And so Aristotle discovered, or pretended to discover, that tragedy did certain things to protect itself from being merely cruel. It chose, Aristotle said, a certain kind of hero: he was of a certain social and moral stature; he had a certain degree of possibility of free choice; he must justify his fate, or seem to justify it, by his moral condition, being neither wholly good nor wholly bad, having a particular fault that collaborates with destiny to bring about his ruin. The purpose of all these specifications for the tragic hero is to assure us that we observe something more than mere passivity when we witness the hero's suffering, that the suffering has, as we say, some meaning, some show of rationality.

Aristotle's theory of tragedy has had its way with the world to an extent which is perhaps out of proportion to its comprehensiveness and accuracy. Its success is largely due to its having dealt so openly with the paradox of tragedy. It serves to explain away any guilty feelings that we may have at deriving pleasure from suffering.

But at the same time that the world has accepted Aristotle's theory of tragedy, it has also been a little uneasy about some of its implications. The element of the theory that causes uneasiness in modern times is the matter of the stature of the hero. To a society based in egalitarian sentiments, the requirement that the hero be a man of rank seems to deny the presumed dignity of tragedy to men of lesser status. And to a culture which questions the freedom of the will, Aristotle's hero seems to be a little beside the point. Aristotle's prescription for the tragic hero is clearly connected with his definition, in his *Ethics*, of the nature of an ethical action. He tells us that a truly ethical action must be a free choice between two alternatives. This definition is then wonderfully complicated by a further requirement—that the moral man must be so trained in making the right choice that he makes it as a matter of habit, makes it, as it were, instinctively. Yet it *is* a choice, and reason plays a part in its making. But we, of course, don't give to reason the same place in the moral life that Aristotle gave it. And in general, over the last hundred and fifty years, dramatists and novelists have tried their hand at the representation of human suffering without the particular safeguards against cruelty which Aristotle perceived, or contrived. A very large part of the literature of Western Europe may be understood in terms of an attempt to invert or criticize the heroic prescription of the hero, by burlesque and comedy, or by the insistence on the commonplace, the lowering of the hero's social status and the diminution of his power of reasoned choice. The work of Fielding may serve as an example of how the mind of Europe has been haunted by the great image of classical tragedy, and how it has tried to lay that famous ghost. When Fielding calls his hero Tom Jones, he means that his young man is not Orestes or Achilles; when he calls him a foundling, he is suggesting that Tom Jones is not, all appearances to the contrary notwithstanding, Oedipus.

Edith Wharton was following where others led. Her impulse in conceiving the story of Ethan Frome was not, however, that of moral experimentation. It was, as I have said, a purely literary impulse, in the bad sense of the word "literary." Her aim is not that of Wordsworth in any of his stories of the suffering poor, to require of us that we open our minds to a realization of the kinds of people whom suffering touches. Nor is it that of Flaubert in *Madame Bovary*, to wring from solid circumstances all the pity and terror of an ancient tragic fable. Nor is it that of Dickens or Zola, to shake us with the perception of social injustice, to instruct us in the true nature of social life and to dispose us to indignant opinion and action. These are not essentially literary intentions; they are moral intentions. But all that Edith Wharton has in mind is to achieve that grim tableau of which I have spoken, of pain and imprisonment, of life-in-death. About the events that lead up to this tableau, there is nothing she finds to say, nothing whatever. The best we can conclude of the meaning of her story is that it might perhaps be a subject of discourse in the context of rural sociology—it might be understood to exemplify the thesis that love and joy do not flourish on poverty-stricken New England farms. If we try to bring it into the context of morality, its meaning goes no further than certain cultural considerations—that is, to people who like their literature to show the "smiling aspects of life," it may be thought to say, "This is the aspect that life really has, as grim as this"; while to people who repudiate a literature that represents only the smiling aspects of life it says, "How intelligent and how brave you are to be able to understand that life is as grim as this." It is really not very much to say.

And yet there is in *Ethan Frome* an idea of considerable importance. It is there by reason of the author's deficiencies, not by reason of her powers—because it suits Edith Wharton's rather dull intention to be content with telling a story about people who do not make moral decisions, whose fate cannot have moral reverberations. The idea is this: that moral inertia, the *not* making of moral decisions, constitutes a large part of the moral life of humanity.

This isn't an idea that literature likes to deal with. Literature is charmed by energy and dislikes inertia. It characteristically represents morality as positive action. The same is true of the moral philosophy of the West—has been true ever since Aristotle defined a truly moral act by its energy of reason, of choice. A later development of this tendency said that an act was really moral only if it went against the inclination of the person performing the act: the idea was parodied as saying that one could not possibly act morally to one's friends, only to one's enemies.

Yet the dull daily world sees something below this delightful preoccupation of literature and moral philosophy. It is aware of the morality of inertia, and of its function as a social base, as a social cement. It knows that duties are done for no other reason than that they are said to be duties; for no other reason, sometimes, than that the doer has not really been able to conceive of any other course—has, perhaps, been afraid to think of any other course. Hobbes said of the Capitol geese that saved Rome by their cackling that they were the salvation of the city, not because they were they but there. How often the moral act is performed not because we are we but because we are there! This is the morality of habit, or the morality of biology. This is Ethan Frome's morality, simple, unquestioning,

passive, even masochistic. His duties as a son are discharged because
he is a son; his duties as a husband are discharged because he is
a husband. He does nothing by moral election. At one point in his
story he is brought to moral crisis—he must choose between his
habituated duty to his wife and his duty and inclination to the girl
he loves. It is quite impossible for him to deal with the dilemma in
the high way that literature and moral philosophy prescribe, by reason and choice. Choice is incompatible with his idea of his existence;
he can only elect to die.

Literature, of course, is not wholly indifferent to what I have
called the morality of habit and biology, the morality of inertia. But
literature, when it deals with this morality, is tempted to qualify its
dullness by endowing it with a certain high grace. There is never
any real moral choice for the Félicité of Flaubert's story "A Simple
Heart." She is all pious habit of virtue, and of blind, unthinking,
unquestioning love. There are, of course, such people as Félicité,
simple, good, loving—quite stupid in their love, not choosing where
to bestow it. We meet such people frequently in literature, in the
pages of Balzac, Dickens, Dostoevsky, Joyce, Faulkner, Hemingway.
They are of a quite different order of being from those who try the
world with their passion and their reason; they are by way of being
saints, of the less complicated kind. They do not really exemplify
what I mean by the morality of inertia. Literature is uncomfortable
in the representation of the morality of inertia or of biology, and
overcomes its discomfort by representing it with the added grace of
that extravagance which we denominate saintliness.

But the morality of inertia is to be found in very precise exempli-
fication in one of Wordsworth's poems. Wordsworth is preëminent
among the writers who experimented in the representation of new
kinds and bases of moral action—he has a genius for imputing moral
existence to people who, according to the classical morality, should
have no moral life at all. And he has the courage to make this im-
putation without at the same time imputing the special grace and
interest of saintliness. The poem I have in mind is ostensibly about
a flower, but the transition from the symbol to the human fact is
clearly, if awkwardly, made. The flower is a small celandine, and the
poet observes that it has not, in the natural way of flowers, folded
itself against rough weather:

But lately, one rough day, this Flower I passed
And recognized it, though in altered form,
Now standing as an offering to the blast,
And buffeted at will by rain and storm.

I stopped, and said with inly-muttered voice,
It doth not love the shower nor seek the cold;
This neither is its courage nor its choice,
But its necessity in being old.

Neither courage nor choice, but necessity: it cannot do otherwise. Yet it acts as if by courage and choice. This is the morality imposed by brute circumstance, by biology, by habit, by the unspoken social demand which we have not the strength to refuse, or, often, to imagine refusing. People are scarcely ever praised for living according to this morality—we do not suppose it to be a morality at all until we see it being broken.

This is morality as it is conceived by the great mass of people in the world. And with this conception of morality goes the almost entire negation of any connection between morality and destiny. A superstitious belief in retribution may play its part in the thought of simple people, but essentially they think of catastrophes as fortuitous, without explanation, without reason. They live in the moral universe of the Book of Job. In complex lives, morality does in some part determine destiny; in most lives it does not. Between the moral life of Ethan and Mattie and their terrible fate we cannot make any reasonable connection. Only a moral judgment cruel to the point of insanity could speak of it as anything but accidental.

I have not spoken of the morality of inertia in order to praise it but only to recognize it, to suggest that when we keep our minds fixed on what the great invigorating books tell us about the moral life, we obscure the large bulking dull mass of moral fact. Morality is not only the high, torturing dilemmas of Ivan Karamazov and Captain Vere. It is also the deeds performed without thought, without choice, perhaps even without love, as Zeena Frome ministers to Ethan and Mattie. The morality of inertia, of the dull, unthinking round of duties, may, and often does, yield the immorality of inertia; the example that will most readily occur to us is that of the good simple people, so true to their family responsibilities, who gave no

thought to the concentration camps in whose shadow they lived. No:
the morality of inertia is not to be praised, but it must be recognized.
And Edith Wharton's little novel must be recognized for bringing
to our attention what we, and literature, so easily forget.

On *The Reef*: A Letter

by Henry James

[Mrs. Wharton had sent him her recently published novel, *The Reef*.]

Dictated.

Lamb House, Rye.
December 4th, 1912.

My dear E. W.

Your beautiful book has been my portion these several days, but as other matters, of a less ingratiating sort, have shared the fair harbourage, I fear I have left it a trifle bumped and *bousculé* in that at the best somewhat agitated basin. There it will gracefully ride the waves, however, long after every other temporarily floating object shall have sunk, as so much comparative "rot," beneath them. This is a rude figure for my sense of the entire interest and charm, the supreme validity and distinction, of *The Reef*. I am even yet, alas, in anything but a good way—so abominably does my ailment drag itself out; but it has been a real lift to read you and taste and ponder you; the experience has literally worked, at its hours, in a medicating sense that neither my local nor my London Doctor (present here in his greatness for a night and a day) shall have come within miles and miles of. Let me mention at once, and have done with it, that the advent and the effect of the intenser London light can only be described as an anticlimax, in fact as a tragic farce, of the first water; in short one of those *mauvais* tours, as far as results are concerned, that make one wonder how a Patient ever survives *any* relation with a Doctor. My Visitor was charming, intelligent, kind, all visibly a great master of the question; but he prescribed me a remedy, to begin its action directly he had left, that simply and at a short notice sent me down into hell, where I lay sizzling (never such a sizzle before) for three days, and has since followed it up with another under the dire effect of which I languish even as I now write. . . . So much to express both what I owe you or *have* owed you at moments that at all lent themselves—in the way of pervading balm, and to explain at the same time how scantly I am able for the hour to make my right acknowledgment.

There are fifty things I should like to say to you about the Book, and I shall have said most of them in the long run; but there are some that eagerly rise to my lips even now and for which I want the benefit of my "first flush" of appreciation. The whole of the finest part is, I think, quite the finest thing you have done; both *more* done than even the best of your other doing, and more worth it through intrinsic value, interest and beauty.

December 9th. I had to break off the other day, my dear Edith, through simple extremity of woe; and the woe has continued unbroken ever since—I have been in bed and in too great suffering, too unrelieved and too continual, for me to attempt any decent form of expression. I have just got up, for one of the first times, even now, and I sit in command of this poor little situation, ostensibly, instead of simply being bossed by it, though I don't at all know what it will bring. To attempt in this state to rise to any worthy reference to *The Reef* seems to me a vain thing; yet there remains with me so strongly the impression of its quality and of the unspeakably *fouillée* nature of the situation between the two principals (more gone into and with more undeviating truth than anything you have done) that I can't but babble of it a little to you even with these weak lips. It all shows, partly, what strength of subject is, and how it carries and inspires, inasmuch as I think your subject in its essence [is] very fine and takes in no end of beautiful things to do. Each of these two figures is admirable for truth and *justesse;* the woman an exquisite thing, and with her characteristic finest, scarce differentiated notes (that is some of them) sounded with a wonder of delicacy. I'm not sure her oscillations are not beyond our notation; yet they are so held in your hand, so felt and known and shown, and

everything seems so to come of itself. I suffer or worry a little from
the fact that in the Prologue, as it were, we are admitted so much
into the consciousness of the man, and that after the introduction of
Anna (Anna so perfectly named) we see him almost only as she sees
him—which gives our attention a different sort of work to do; yet
this is really, I think, but a triumph of your method, for he remains
of an absolute consistent verity, showing himself in that way better
perhaps than in any other, and without a false note imputable, not
a shadow of one, to his manner of so projecting himself. The beauty
of it is that it is, for all it is worth, a Drama, and almost, as it seems
to me, of the psychologic Racinian unity, intensity and gracility.
Anna is really of Racine and one presently begins to feel her
throughout as an Eriphyle or a Bérénice: which, by the way, helps
to account a little for something *qui me chiffonne* throughout:
which is why the whole thing, unrelated and unreferred save in the
most superficial way to its *milieu* and background, and to any de-
termining or qualifying *entourage,* takes place *comme cela,* and in
a specified, localised way, in France—these non-French people "elect-
ing," as it were, to have their story out there. This particularly makes
all sorts of unanswered questions come up about Owen; and the
notorious wickedness of Paris isn't at all required to bring about
the conditions of the Prologue. Oh, if you knew how plentifully we
could supply them in London and, I should suppose, in New York
or in Boston. But the point was, as I see it, that you couldn't really
give us the sense of a Boston Eriphyle or Boston Givré, and that an
exquisite instinct, "back of" your Racinian inspiration and settling
the whole thing for you, whether consciously or not, absolutely prescribed a vague and elegant French colonnade or gallery, with a
French river dimly gleaming through, as the harmonious *fond* you
required. In the key of this, with all your reality, you have yet kept
the whole thing: and, to deepen the harmony and accentuate the
literary pitch, have never surpassed yourself for certain exquisite
moments, certain images, analogies, metaphors, certain silver cor-
respondences in your *façon de dire;* examples of which I could pluck
out and numerically almost confound you with, were I not stammer-
ing this in so handicapped a way. There used to be little notes in
you that were like fine benevolent finger-marks of the good George
Eliot—the echo of much reading of that excellent woman, here and

there, that is, sounding through. But now you are like a lost and recovered "ancient" whom *she* might have got a reading of (especially were he a Greek) and of whom in *her* texture some weaker reflection were to show. For, dearest Edith, you are stronger and firmer and finer than all of them put together; you go further and you say *mieux*, and your only drawback is not having the homeliness and the inevitability and the happy limitation and the affluent poverty, of a Country of your Own (*comme moi, par exemple!*) It makes you, this does, as you exquisitely say of somebody or something at some moment, elegiac (what penetration, what delicacy in your use there of the term!)—makes you so, that is, for the Racinian-*sérieux*—but leaves you more in the desert (for everything else) that surrounds Apex City. But you will say that you're content with your lot; that the desert surrounding Apex City is quite enough of a dense crush for you, and that with the *colonnade* and the gallery and the dim river you will always otherwise pull through. To which I can only assent—after such an example of pulling through as *The Reef*. Clearly you have only to pull, and everything will come.

These are tepid and vain remarks, for truly I am helpless. I have had all these last days a perfect hell of an exasperation of my dire complaint, the 11th week of which begins to-day, and have arrived at the point really—the weariness of pain so great—of not knowing *à quel saint me vouer*. In this despair, and because "change" at any hazard and any cost is strongly urged upon me by both my Doctors, and is a part of the regular process of *dénouement* of my accursed ill, I am in all probability trying to scramble up to London by the end of this week, even if I have to tumble, howling, out of bed and go forth in my bedclothes. I shall go in this case to Garlant's Hotel, Suffolk Street, where you have already seen me, and not to my Club, which is impossible in illness, nor to my little flat (21 Carlyle Mansions, Cheyne Walk, Chelsea, S.W.) which will not yet, or for another three or four weeks, be ready for me. The change to London may possibly do something toward breaking the spell: please pray hard that it shall. Forgive too my muddled accents and believe me, through the whole bad business, not the less faithfully yours,

Henry James

Our Literary Aristocrat

by Vernon L. Parrington

The note of distinction is as natural to Edith Wharton as it is rare in our present day literature. She belongs to the "quality," and the grand manner is hers by right of birth. She is as finished as a Sheraton sideboard, and with her poise, grace, high standards, and perfect breeding, she suggests as inevitably old wine and slender decanters. The severe ethical code which Puritanism has bequeathed to her, and the keen intellect which has made her a critical analyst, increase her native distinction; and the irony that plays lambently over her commentary, adds piquancy to her art. She belongs to an earlier age, before a strident generation had come to deny the excellence of standards. No situation which she has conceived in her novels is so ironical as the situation in which she herself is placed; shaken out of an unquestioned acceptance of the aristocratic world to which she belongs, she turns her keen analysis upon her environment, and satirizes what in her heart she loves most.

The Age of Innocence is perfect Whartonian. It is historical satire done with immaculate art, but though she laughs at the deification of "form" by the van der Luydens of Skuytercliff, and the tyranny of their rigid social taboos, she loves them too well to suffer them to be forgotten by a careless generation. She has painted them at full length, to hang upon our walls, where they lend historical dignity to the background of the present and utter a silent reproof to our scrambling vulgarities. New York society of the 1870's, with its little clan of first families that gently simmers in its own dullness—it would be inelegant to say stews—provides a theme that exactly suits Mrs. Wharton's talent. She delights in the make-believe of the clan,

"Our Literary Aristocrat." From *The Pacific Review*, June 1921. Reprinted by permission of V. L. Parrington, Jr.

in "the Pharisaic voice of a society wholly absorbed in barricading itself against the unpleasant," and she half regrets an age whose innocence "seals the mind against imagination and the heart against experience." She herself, of course, will not defend herself against reality by a decorous denial, but she likes too well many things in that world to be harsh or angry with it. Against this background of the clan she projects three figures who come perilously near to realizing a quite vulgar situation. Between May Welland, physically magnificent but mentally equipped with no more than the clan negations, and Ellen Olenska, a clan member who has freed herself from its provincialisms by a European experience that ends in separation from her Polish husband, and whose "disgrace" rocks New York society till the clan rallies to her defense, stands Newland Archer, a third member of the clan, who has played with books and ideas without liberating his mind, who is shocked into naturalness by the more vital Ellen, endeavors to break the ties of clan convention, but is held fast and ends his rebellions in a mood of ironic abnegation. There are no scenes, no vulgar jealousies or accusations, nothing to offend the finest sensibility. A few frank phrases sound almost startling in their context of reticent pretense, but they do not really startle. The book unwinds slowly, somewhat meagerly, with much analysis and little vivacity of conversation. In an environment of dull and selfish respectability, how could there be vivacity; with no ideas, no spontaneity, no intellectual sincerity, it is idle to expect vivacity. The formal routine and hinting gossip wrap themselves like a boa constrictor about the characters and squeeze the naturalness out of them. Nevertheless the story never lags and is never dull. The skill with which dullness is made interesting is a triumph of art.

But when one has said that the craftsmanship is a very great success, why not go further and add that it doesn't make the slightest difference whether one reads the book or not, unless one is a literary epicure who lives for the savor of things. What do the van der Luydens matter to us; or what did they or their kind matter a generation ago? Why waste such skill upon such insignificant material? There were vibrant realities in the New York of the Seventies, Commodore Vanderbilt, for example, or even Jay Gould or Jim Fiske. If Mrs. Wharton had only chosen to throw such figures upon her canvas, brutal, cynical, dominating, what a document of American history —but the suggestion is foolish. Mrs. Wharton could not do it. Her distinction is her limitation. She loathes the world of Jim Fiske too much to understand it. She is too well bred to be a snob, but she escapes it only by sheer intelligence. The background of her mind, the furniture of her habits, are packed with potential snobbery, and it is only by scrupulous care that it is held in leash. She is unconsciously shut in behind plate glass, where butlers serve formal dinners, and white shoulders go up at the mere suggestion of everyday gingham. She belongs in spite of herself to the caste which she satirizes, and she cannot make herself at home in households where the mother washes the dishes and the father tends the furnace. If she had lived less easily, if she had been forced to skimp and save and plan, she would have been a greater and richer artist, more significant because more native, more continental. But unfortunately her doors open only to the smart set; the windows from which she surveys life open only to the east, to London, Paris, Rome. She is one of our cosmopolitans, flitting lightly about and at ease with all who bear titles. And this the stay-at-home American secretly resents. What are titles to him, and for that matter, what are the vulgar rich of New York? Let the newspapers exploit them, for that becomes their vulgarity. But for Mrs. Wharton to spend her talents upon rich nobodies is no less than sheer waste.

Since we are quarreling with Mrs. Wharton let us go through with it and suggest another irritation that arises from less creditable, but quite human sources. She unconsciously irritates because she reveals so unobtrusively how much she knows and how perfect is her breeding. She pricks one's complacency with such devastating certainty; reveals so cruelly one's plebeian limitations. Her readers are always on pins and needles not to appear out of her class. It is impossible to be easy and slouchy in presence of her poise, and it is hard on us not to let down occasionally. We cannot always be mentally on the alert. It was inevitable, to fall back upon an illustration, that her dilettante hero should have gone in for Eastlake furniture, as Mrs. Wharton assures us that he did. But the easy way in which she assumes that the reader will understand her casual reference to Sir Charles's endeavor to revive a "sincere" furniture, puts one to scrambling to recall that Eastlakeism was the polite counterpart, in

the Seventies, of the robust rebellions of William Morris against a
dowdy Victorianism. If Mrs. Wharton had only let slip the fact
that she once wrote a book on household decoration, and "got up"
on the Eastlake movement, it would have reassured us, and made us
feel that she is a common mortal like the rest of us who have to
"get up" on things. Which criticism, of course, arises from mere
petulancy and self-conceit.

With her ripe culture, her clear and clean intelligence, her classical
spirit, her severe standards and austere ethics, Mrs. Wharton is our
outstanding literary aristocrat. She has done notable things, but she
has paid a great price in aloofness from her own America. There
is more hope for our literature in the honest crudities of the younger
naturalists, than in her classic irony; they at least are trying to
understand America as it is. "You'll never amount to anything, any
of you, till you roll up your sleeves and get right down into the
muck," commented the one plebeian in the book to Newland
Archer, who "mentally shrugged his shoulders and turned the conversation to books." Mrs. Wharton too often mentally shrugs her
shoulders over America. That she should ever roll up her sleeves
and get down into the muck is unthinkable.

What Edith Wharton Saw in Innocence

by Louis O. Coxe

It seems unlikely that in putting down my feelings about *The Age of Innocence* I will entirely escape the charge—always justified —of prejudice. One tends in criticism to use a work or a writer as a stick with which to beat other works and writers—or, worse still, other critics—with the result that the book one is concerned with rather escapes. This danger looms larger in the case of the best known novels and poems, those works which have created schools, reputations, endowed chairs, and new stacks in libraries. I have no such oppressive imminence above me in this instance. We all await the release, a few years hence, of Edith Wharton's private papers, and although most students of American literature know the Wharton name and may have read *Ethan Frome*, too few seem to have become acquainted with the entire reach of her work, much of which, one has to confess at once, has value only for the specialist. *The Age of Innocence* has been variously judged, and one of the more recent critics of Edith Wharton places it rather lower than *The House of Mirth*, a judgment with which I disagree, largely, in this instance, because I think the critic seriously misreads the novel.

But all such matters apart, one still has the problem of telling readers, some in the know, some outside, just what it is that strikes one as distinctive and impressive about the book. How to get the reader to go back to *The Age of Innocence* convinced of pleasure and profit to come? Times and readers change but this novel, written at the height of Edith Wharton's powers, retains a power the gradual release of which one becomes aware of with time, with acquaintance, with a more delicate attuning of the ear and the sensibility to the things Edith Wharton was writing about. And it seems to me one of the graces and delights of *The Age of Innocence* lies exactly in the multifariousness of its thematic material, in its refusal to tie itself down to "meaning," the while that it glitters with a density, a hardness of surface that only a truly novelistic eye could have seen and an informing mind recreate.

The seeing is the thing. What does Conrad say? "It is above all to make you *see* . . . and it is everything." I know of no other American novelist with Edith Wharton's power (in this book, at any rate) of simple vision, of showing us who was there and in what grouping, what juxtapositions. The very opening moment of the novel serves as an example: the scene at the opera. Newland Archer and his beautifully dressed, languidly self-assured companions, the tenor and the soprano on the ornate stage, May Welland all in white and pink. Then the entrance into the Mingott box of the Countess Olenska, the dark lady of this plot! Nowhere does Edith Wharton's grip relax; her hold on actuality is everywhere firm. She has been there—she knows. From the smallest flower in the Beaufort conservatory to the styling of dresses by Worth in the Seventies— she knows it all and she knows how to put it before us in all its appeal of the rare, the far-off, the perhaps absurd. And in so doing, she does not patronize either her readers or her characters and their world; in fact, the irony cuts several ways at once, with the result that those of us who succumb to the temptation of contempt for fashionable New York society in the Seventies get our comeuppance; she does not flatter us with the delusion that we have progressed or found a new freedom. We have simply changed masters.

The scenes that strike us so vividly throughout the novel are of different sorts, and not one seems there for its own sake. The wonderfully vivid tableau of May Welland, the still glowing, Dianaesque matron on the lawn at Newport, bow at shoulder, while the rosy girls watch her marksmanship and the idle gentlemen assess the ladies and their quality—surely no delight in mere grouping and bric-a-brac, though such delight is legitimate on the author's part and ours, but a lively sense of surface and attitude, without which no deeper probing is possible. And the probing takes us deep enough for comfort, down to the quick of a society, a world, a whole history of the American sensibility.   *theme*

That indeed seems to emerge as the finest quality of Edith Wharton's theme in *The Age of Innocence,* the whole question of the old and the new, of passion and duty, of the life of the feelings and that of the senses. For us, reading the book some decades after its publication, the complexities of meaning alone make the novel seem far richer than many another more highly touted. And again, here is no apparatus composed of symbols, near-allegory and didacticism, but a tissue of objects, places, attitudes, and desires.

If one can plump for a single "meaning" that the book may hold for us today, it may well be that of the lost life of feeling, the kind of life, the kinds of feeling, that Newland Archer's son seems utterly incapable of understanding or knowing. At the very end, when Newland Archer, for the last time, retreats from Ellen Olenska and from the sort of experience his son Dallas is only too glad to meet, we feel the fullness of the irony. Archer, with his insecurity, his sensitivity, and his passion has obeyed the moral imperatives of his class and time and has given up Ellen and love for the furtherance of the shallow-seeming aims, all amorphous as they are, of his world. He has stuck to May and to his New York, giving up another world.

What has he got in return? Another writer would perhaps say, quite simply: "Nothing," and indict the time and himself along with it, but of course to Edith Wharton "everything is true in a different sense." What Newland has lost is not Ellen, but May, whom he never took pains to know or to love, May who knew all along the extent and the fullness of her husband's "sacrifice." That the first inkling Archer gains of this should come from the casual, almost flippant, remarks of his son Dallas adds another twist to the ironic knot. What does Dallas know of the life of the feelings and passions, he who has always known who he is, what he wants, where he is going? He has only to ask and it is straightaway made clear to him: "What's the use of making mysteries?" says Dallas. "It only makes people want to nose 'em out." And we quite agree, knowing with our unerring hindsight that the best that can be said for Dallas' world is that he and his fellows knew not what mysteries they made, whereas Archer and his contemporaries most certainly did. For Dallas it would have been so simple: run away with Ellen Olenska and hang what people will say. It is no longer necessary for him to run and scandalize in order that he may enjoy Fanny

Beaufort. Times have changed, and in this simpler and freer world
of Dallas' young manhood, there are no occasions to exercise the
feelings nor nourish passion. Like every son who ever was, he can
see in the married life of his parents only the grim, the incommunicable, the faintly ludicrous:

> ". . . you date, you see, dear old boy. But mother said . . ."
> "Your mother?"
> "Yes: the day before she died. It was when she sent for me alone—
> you remember? She said she knew we were safe with you and always
> would be, because once, when she asked you to, you'd given up the
> thing you most wanted."
> Archer received this communication in silence. . . . At length he
> said in a low voice: "She never asked me."
> "No. I forgot. You never did ask each other anything, did you?
> And you never told each other anything. You just sat and watched
> each other, and guessed at what was going on underneath. A deaf-
> and-dumb asylum, in fact! Well, I back your generation for knowing
> more about each other's private thoughts than we ever have time to
> find out about our own. —I say, Dad," Dallas broke off, "you're not
> angry with me? If you are, let's make it up and go and lunch at
> Henri's. I've got to rush out to Versailles afterward."

For Dallas, it is just that simple—and what a knot of irony has
tightened in this brief passage! Can Dallas or anyone like him begin
to understand the meaning of the kind of feelings Archer has known?
Have they the time? the imagination? the passion? What can the
notion of a buried life mean to one who can conceive only of surface? As Archer himself puts it to himself, "the thing one's so certain
of in advance: can it ever make one's heart beat wildly?"

Newland Archer does not say this to his son. Times have changed
and the steady cultivation of the affections, of nuances of feeling
which only an ordered society allows seems to the new generation "a
deaf and dumb asylum." Dallas and his contemporaries have a
kindly contempt for such old-fashioned, illiberal notions, would
throw down all the canons by which a rigid society governed its
members. Archer, who sees that "there [is] good in the new order
too" still asks:

> What was left of the little world he had grown up in, and whose
> standards had bent and bound him?

And again:

> "That's it: they [Dallas' generation] feel equal to things—they know their way about," he mused, thinking of his son as the spokesman of the new generation which had swept away all the old landmarks, and with them the sign posts and the danger-signals.

And the danger signal! The innocence of Newland Archer, to think that the society of which he was a part could set and keep the life it sought—could hold it, make it last, by occasional raids on dissenters and backsliders by the van der Luydens, come down in all their minatory splendor from Skuytercliff—to keep offenders in line! All dreadfully amusing—and yet . . . And yet the innocence of Dallas to propose remaking the world and human nature—to think that to cast off one form of bondage means freedom.

Here (one hesitates on the threshold of sociology) we are back at the Americanism of our novel and the old saw of American innocence, the curious underside of it that the novelists (the best of them) alone can show us. What we have here in Newland Archer is but Lambert Strether seen from another point of view—and from both points he figures as American. My lost youth. Lost, all lost. The discovery, too late, that what one had known as final is all too patently, seen from here and now, no such matter. If James would in some sort show us that America is too simple, too unknowing, Edith Wharton seems to be saying that only if America can evolve a society which feels deeply and can say what it feels can it do more than shift from generation to generation, without a sense of the past, without depth, without blessing. What to feel with and about, we wonder, contemplating the prospect. *The Age of Innocence* makes this clear enough, I think, to us who have rather more sense of what the Dallases of the twentieth century have got us into, all innocent as they were. The total commitment of May to her world and to Newland Archer: is there nothing admirable in this? Nothing of the heroic? For I believe that if any character in this novel partakes of the heroic nature, it is indeed May Welland, she of the pink and white surface and the candid glance, whose capacity for passion and sacrifice her husband never knew. And—irony again—her son Dallas sees it all so clearly, but it is to him "prehistoric," "dated." The innocence of May Welland, so perfectly adjusted to her society, so much a product of "race, moment, milieu," takes on at least a kind of grandeur which, if we put any stock at all these days in the uncommon, approaches the tragic.

Edith Wharton is very clear about all of this: she opposes Archer, the near-rebel, with May, the total conformist. Here a lesser novelist would have been content to rest, in the mere showing of the processes by which an American with separatist tendencies is broken to harness and curb. That she does not leave it at this adds dimension to the book and to the novelist's vision. The emphasis here rests finally upon the ways in which an individual, in more or less settled times, can come to identify his illusions with those of his world. The rightness or wrongness of such identification we may determine if we can, though for my part I would say that the triumph of Edith Wharton's realism strikes one as most sweeping in just her very refusal to draw any such line: she seems merely to say, that is the way things were for these people. Had you done differently, it would have been a different time, place and cast.

If this novel is not quite a retelling of *Bérénice* there is in it some, at least, of Racine's sense of fatality and of the course of duty as a form of fate to be defied at one's peril. As Archer quite clearly sees, to follow one's simple duty means that one must in some sense lose one's life. Yet this is not really the tragedy for Archer; it comes at last, as we have seen, to his final inability to see that if he cannot —must not—have Ellen and the rich life of "Europe," he still has May. But having once had a vision of Ellen Olenska and her passion, May, the white and conventional counterpart of Ellen, must figure to him as the embodiment of the society that denies the vision's fulfillment. It is not so, of course. With his careful, lifelong cultivation of the sensibilities and the passions, Newland Archer has unfitted himself for passionate, devoted action. May has the last word. How rich in its suffering and incommunicable love must have been her buried life! And that very capacity to feel and to suffer serves as a cousinly and female bond between May and Ellen. Archer, the object of two such loves, has never been able to take the risk of either.

What a waste! Is that what one says on finishing the book? Perhaps. All that wasted emotion, feeling, suffering. All that past blotted out by change and the nice detergent of the new generation. In a sense, America *is* waste, as Edith Wharton very well knew—wasteful of its past, that greatest of resources. Yet we today, who have perhaps a nostalgia for such past times as that Edith Wharton dwells on, would do well to realize how supremely well she makes us heirs and possessors of that long-ago world. If the backward longing for the Twenties Fitzgerald provoked and could not satisfy came to nothing, it may be that another novelist shall one day possess it for us, as Hawthorne possessed for us the New England of our inescapable origins. Bit by bit they will piece our American grand tour together, the novelists. We may very well not like what we find. But when we do find it—not complete but moving—we shall give Edith Wharton more of her due than she has yet received. Beyond that, and there really are things and places beyond America, we can do honor to one of the fine novels of our century. We can try to read it.

On *The Age of Innocence*

by *Blake Nevius*

. . . In *The Age of Innocence* (1920) Mrs. Wharton's recoil from the postwar world is felt mainly by indirection, in her choice of setting. Although it is clear that like her hero, Newland Archer, who "cherished his old New York even when he smiled at it," she could reconcile two points of view, the indictment outweighs the defense. In her protest against the deliberately nurtured innocence of old New York, she continued in *The Age of Innocence*—as she had done before in *The Reef* and *Ethan Frome*—to rehearse her own complaint against the failures of education and opportunity that had hampered her growth as a human being and as an artist. But underlying her protest was the nostalgia evoked by the setting and manners familiar to her childhood, a nostalgia that was to grow with the years until it effaced what bitterness remained.

"Unconsciously to us all," one of Edith Wharton's old friends has written in Lubbock's memoir, "life began to change from simplicity to vulgarity somewhere in the late Eighties." Significantly, the setting of *The Age of Innocence* antedates that minor social revolution. Although the storm warnings were up, for those who cared to heed them, the mercantile aristocracy in the Seventies was for the most part impregnable in its complacency. Julius Beaufort, the beefy financier of *The Age of Innocence*, is a disturbing portent, but his financial disgrace only strengthens Washington Square in its self-esteem. Ellen Olenska, who represents another kind of threat to the tribal security, is vanquished when society closes about the Newland Archers like a Roman wall. What one notices about this little world is that it is hermetically sealed against contamination. The question that arises with respect to such novels as *The Fruit of the Tree, A Son at the Front,* and *Hudson River Bracketed*—to what extent was Edith Wharton competent to deal with social and political issues beyond her limited perspective?—is as irrelevant in this instance as it would be for Jane Austen. Nothing in her treatment is more truly representative than its exclusions. We may listen in vain for echoes from the outside world. The crude, boisterous spectacle of postwar expansion, featured by the corruptions of the Grant regime, the rapid extension of the frontier, and the problems posed by labor, immigration, and urbanization, fails to penetrate the consciousness of old New York or to modify in any way its timeless ritual. Never before had Edith Wharton succeeded so well in adapting her subject to her limitations while at the same time allowing full scope for her talents.

There is some advantage to be gained from reading *A Backward Glance* as a preface to *The Age of Innocence,* if only to be assured where to locate the novel's emphasis and to be able to trace the origin of some of Mrs. Wharton's most successful details. Although there is a wealth of minor parallels—for example, the old Newbold Madeira, famous in its day, has become "the old Lanning Port," and the great-grandfather of the novelist, General Ebenezer Stevens, who directed the surrender of Burgoyne after Saratoga, has become one of Newland Archer's distinguished ancestors—the general parallels are more helpful. The salient peculiarities of the age of innocence are plainly marked in both. The society reproduced in the novel consisted of a small number of families, ranked in a strict angelic hierarchy according to ancestry and financial means—qualifications which held good only so long as one did not enter retail business, exhibit any form of personal or financial dishonesty, or elope with the first maid or chauffeur. In the Seventies money was still unable to purchase entrance into the charmed circle; in fact, the mere mention of it was distasteful. The young men had no active interest in adding to their capital. They lived off the enterprise of their forebears and the profits realized from the boom in New York real estate values. None of them, as Edith Wharton recalled, was "in business."

They were trained to be lawyers or bankers or stockbrokers, but, like Newland Archer and Ralph Marvell, they kept no office hours and their profession was mainly an ornament.

"It is a singular fact," Henry James remarked of Newport, "that a society that does nothing is decidedly more pictorial, more interesting to the eye of contemplation, than a society which is hard at work." Edith Wharton would have agreed. It was precisely this pictorial quality that attracted her and enabled her to demonstrate once again that she had the "visualizing power" beyond any other novelist of her time. In the intervals between shooting, fishing, and boat racing, the male members of this society lent themselves agreeably to the social strategies of their women. It was a society not merely ingrown, but, judging from the novel, strongly matriarchal, in which the real authority was exerted—blatantly or quietly, and on descending levels—by Mrs. van der Luyden, Mrs. Manson Mingott, and the elder Mrs. Archer. One is reminded, in fact, of the similar view we get of aristocratic French society in the novels of both James and Mrs. Wharton. There too we encounter the formidable old dowagers, narrowly devoted to the ideal of *la famille* and, secondly, the clan, and managing, like the Duchess in *The American* or the Marquise de Malrives in *Madame de Treymes*, to symbolize with immense force the authority residing in the concept of a traditional society. One may even be struck by the unconscious identification which Edith Wharton makes between the Marquise de Malrives and her circle, "who mostly bore the stamp of personal insignificance on their mildly sloping or aristocratically beaked faces," and the Archer women, "tall, pale, and slightly round-shouldered, with long noses, sweet smiles and a kind of drooping distinction like that in certain faded Reynolds portraits."

Edith Wharton's final, balanced judgment of old New York, notably less severe than her earlier judgment, appears in *A Backward Glance* and has been noted frequently. Its virtues, as she saw them, were "social amenity and financial incorruptibility"; its defects were principally two: "an instinctive shrinking from responsibility" and "a blind dread of innovation." Although the positive values represented by this narrow segment of American society are implied in *The Age of Innocence*, its failures are more apparent. Its members were the descendants of Hamilton's Federalists, but they had no discernible interest in politics. Following the Civil War, some of these leisured gentlemen began to interest themselves in municipal affairs to the extent of serving on the boards of museums, libraries, and charities, but beyond this they could not bring themselves to go. Politics was out of bounds; consequently, Mrs. Wharton explained, "none of my friends rendered the public service that a more enlightened social system would have exacted of them." Perhaps she was thinking of England, where the best—and sometimes the worst—abilities of the nobility were enlisted in the professional branches of government. At any rate, she found a very real criticism of American democracy in its failure to utilize the best material at hand: "In every society there is the room, and the need, for a cultivated leisure class; but from the first the spirit of our institutions has caused us to waste this class instead of using it." This is one of the bitterest comments in *A Backward Glance*, representing the ultimate phase of Edith Wharton's conservatism. In the interval following *The Age of Innocence* she moved from an indictment, however partial, of the class itself to an indictment of the system which first neglected that class and then swallowed it whole. And, curiously, the same contradiction is perpetuated in her memoirs.

It is the "dread of innovation," however, expressed in a thousand forms of resistance, that characterizes old New York most completely. When she is describing her parents' taste in literature, Mrs. Wharton can afford, even in *A Backward Glance*, to be amused. Repeatedly in her stories—in *The Age of Innocence, The Old Maid, Hudson River Bracketed*—she lists the authors, gentlemen all, who were sanctioned by the parlor censor: Irving, Halleck, Drake, and the elder Dana. The more vigorous talents, like Poe and Whitman, who were invariably the more disreputable in their antecedents and associations, were either ignored or dismissed as vulgar. Mrs. Archer and her daughter, whose tastes were identical, "spoke severely of Dickens, who 'had never drawn a gentleman,' and considered Thackeray less at home in the great world than Bulwer." The irony is so unmistakable that one can only smile at the critic who took Mrs. Wharton's reference to Melville in *A Backward Glance* as evidence of her snobbishness ("As for Herman Melville, a cousin of the van Rensselaers, and qualified by birth to figure in the best society, he was doubtless excluded from it by his deplorable Bohemianism, for I never heard his name mentioned, or saw one of his books"). The resistance to literature was, in effect, a resistance to new and unsettling ideas and new forms of experience. When this attitude was extended to the more vital concerns of life, Edith Wharton was no longer amused. There it meant the substitution of an elaborate system of conventions for the natural response to situations. "In reality," Edith Wharton wrote of Newland Archer and his contemporaries, "they all lived in a kind of hieroglyphic world, where the real thing was never said or done or even thought, but only represented by a set of arbitrary signs."

In delineating such a world, the novel of manners is indispensable. The real drama is played out below the surface—the impeccable, sophisticated surface—and communicates itself, if at all, to the observer by means of signs which only the initiate can read. Hence the significance, to old New York, of certain gestures by which the private drama is made public: that frightening portent of social annihilation, the "cut"; the dinner invitation from the van der Luydens, the invitation to occupy a prominent box at the opera, or the presence of Mrs. Manson Mingott's carriage before the door, all signalizing reinstatement; the sudden flight to Europe, which is the solution to every serious emotional crisis. These are the less arbitrary signs. By and large, however, the acquired manners of old New York lend themselves to what Edith Wharton termed "an elaborate system of mystification." A young girl carefully bred in the tradition, like May Welland, knows the social value of the well-timed blush, the feigned reluctance during courtship, and the long engagement. May is so completely the product of the system that Newland Archer, following their marriage, is forced to admit that she will never surprise him "by a new idea, a weakness, a cruelty or an emotion." Thus the problem for the novelist becomes a difficult if engaging one. If passions are to spin the plot with a minimum of labor for himself, they must be visible. If they are not, the novelist may be forced to rely on certain conventions. The detected rendezvous—Selden's glimpse of Lily Bart emerging from the Trenor mansion, or the interview between Ellen Olenska and Newland Archer which is witnessed by the scandal-mongering Larry Lefferts—becomes as necessary to Edith Wharton's art as the overheard conversation and the intercepted letter are to Shakespeare's.

It is difficult to read *The Age of Innocence* without being struck by its resemblance to that earliest of "modern" novels, *The Princess of Clèves,* which has been described by the author of *The Writing of Fiction* as "a story of hopeless love and mute renunciation in which the stately tenor of the lives depicted is hardly ruffled by the exultations and agonies succeeding each other below the surface." Mrs. Wharton might have been describing *The Age of Innocence.* Both novels train their analysis on the effects of unsatisfied passion, and the heroine in each—Madame de Clèves in the first and Ellen Olenska in the second—is a victim of what Nancy Mitford has defined as "the curious shrinking from happiness . . . a state of mind that has been beautifully observed and recorded by Henry James in *The American* as well as, in a more extraverted way, by Balzac in the *Duchesse de Langeais,* and which is to be found among Frenchwomen to this day." More striking than these incidental parallels is the fact that, however corrupt the court of Henry II may appear in contrast to Washington Square, the members of both societies were trained to disguise their feelings, so that in Madame de Lafayette's novel, as in *The Age of Innocence,* the intricate play and counterplay of motives scarcely, as Edith Wharton noted, disturbs the surface.

But *The Princess of Clèves* is distinctly not a novel of manners. To Madame de Lafayette must go the credit for demonstrating more clearly than anyone before her that the novel, as opposed to the drama, is the perfect vehicle for the presentation of an action in which the conflict is profoundly internal, in which, because their situation requires them to assume a mask, almost nothing can be inferred from what the characters do or say—from their gestures, expressions, tones of voice. Madame de Lafayette is preoccupied directly with the psychology of her characters as it reveals itself in consciousness rather than in action. It remained for a Balzac, following in the tradition, but absorbing the contribution of the picaresque novelists, to capitalize on the value of manners as indicating—to use Trilling's phrase again—"the largest intentions of men's souls as well as the smallest." Like Balzac, and unlike Madame de Lafayette, Edith Wharton is a materialist in fiction. Balzac's endless curiosity about the minutiae of business and legal transactions, property rights, and the arts of decoration is almost matched by

Edith Wharton's passion for the detail of costume and decor; and her notation of the manners of her class is as scrupulous as Balzac's notation of bourgeois manners in *César Birotteau* or *Eugénie Grandet*. And both, it might be added, apprehended their characters intellectually. It is difficult to conceive of *The Age of Innocence* ever having been written without the fruitful example of the great French novelist.

   The Age of Innocence is not Mrs. Wharton's strongest novel, but, along with *Ethan Frome*, it is the one in which she is most thoroughly the artist. It is a triumph of style, of the perfect adaptation of means to a conception fully grasped from the outset. It would be difficult to say that she faltered or overreached at any point. The movement of her plot may be established by the successive and clearly marked positions taken by Newland Archer in his relations with Ellen Olenska and May Welland. May Welland personifies all the evasions and compromises of his clan; she is the "safe" alternative; whereas Ellen has the "mysterious faculty of suggesting tragic and moving possibilities outside the daily run of experience." Charmed by May's innocence, and about to announce his engagement to her, Archer at first finds it easy to join old New York in condemning the Mingotts for sponsoring Countess Olenska: "Few things seemed to Newland Archer more awful than an offence against 'Taste,' that far-off divinity of whom 'Form' was the mere visible representative and vice-regent." He is the willing accomplice of a society "wholly absorbed in barricading itself against the unpleasant," and his appreciation of May Welland is based on this precarious ideal: "Nothing about his betrothed pleased him more than her resolute determination to carry to its utmost limits that ritual of ignoring the 'unpleasant' in which they had both been brought up." In the story that follows Edith Wharton tries to make clear what this innocence costs. The measure of change wrought in Archer's outlook by his experience with Ellen is suggested by a sentence occurring midway in the novel, before the echo of his earlier belief has quite died away: "Ah, no, he did not want May to have that kind of innocence, the innocence that seals the mind against imagination and the heart against experience!"

   His fall from grace is carefully motivated. Old New York's treatment of Countess Olenska eventually arouses the innate sense of

chivalry that he shares with Ralph Marvell, and once he has read
the divorce evidence his indifference is vanquished: "she stood before
him as an exposed and pitiful figure, to be saved at all costs from
farther wounding herself in her mad plunges against fate." In spite
of his strict notions, he is not entirely unprepared for a sentimental
adventure. One of the first things we learn about him is that he has
had an affair with a married woman "whose charms had held his
fancy through two mildly agitated years." Once he has accepted
Ellen's case—ironically at the instigation of the clan—he is compelled by logic and sympathy, and finally by the deeper reasons of
love, to adopt her point of view. Nothing in Edith Wharton's treatment of the situation is more subtly expressed than the changes
which Archer's affair with Ellen work in his perceptions. But his
freedom is won too late. Ellen has at the same time learned something from him. She has accepted seriously one of the lessons he had
mastered by rote and passed on to her: that freedom cannot be
purchased at another's cost. It makes no difference that he is now
prepared to discard it. He has given her an idea by which to live
and, in doing so, destroyed the one means of enlarging his new-
found freedom. When he returns to May Welland, it is to the ultimate realization that, like John Marcher in James's "The Beast in
the Jungle," he is the man "to whom nothing was ever to happen."

Edith Wharton never surpassed the irony in which she enveloped
this play of cross-purposes. "It is impossible to be ironical," she
once noted, "without having a sense of the infinitudes." To the
novelist so equipped, the complacent worldliness of old New York
offered fair game. Irony was the method best suited to her temperament and her material. It was her way of telling the world that
she had not been taken in, whatever her allegiances: and it was the
only alternative to tragedy, which, as she suggested in novel after
novel, was impossible in her world. It was an atmosphere, however,
in which a reader such as Katherine Mansfield, for all her admiration of *The Age of Innocence*, found it increasingly difficult to
breathe, for Mrs. Wharton's self-control got on her nerves until she
asked, quite irrelevantly in this instance at least, whether it was
vulgar "to entreat a little wildness, a dark place or two in the soul."

The touch of "wildness" may be lacking, but there is no failure of
sensibility in the novel. The intimate passages between Newland

Archer and Ellen Olenska are as deeply moving as those between
Ethan Frome and Mattie Silver, whose dilemma is so curiously repeated under far different circumstances. The frustration of the
lovers is expressed with great skill by two main devices. Their affair
begins and ends in the glare of publicity, from the moment Archer
sees his countess at the opera to the moment he discovers that old
New York regards them as lovers. The opening chapter of the novel
is superbly conceived from both the novelist's and the social historian's viewpoint. The theater in the Seventies was just in the
process of becoming what it is so clearly today, a social arena in
which private dramas could be effectively highlighted. The scene at
the opera not only introduces the main characters, together with
those secondary characters who will serve as commentators—Siller-
ton Jackson, the undisputed authority on "family," and Lawrence
Lefferts, the arbiter of "form"—but it makes Ellen Olenska a public
issue; it establishes her in a position from which she cannot retreat
and in which she is subject to the maximum scrutiny. The consciousness of this fact, shared by the lovers, makes their every subsequent
encounter a pathetically frustrating one.

The second device I would call attention to is Edith Wharton's
insistence on the chaste, almost palpable barrier which divides the
lovers from the start and which they maintain, even when they are
alone, by the thought of their obligations. Time and again—in
Ellen's drawing room, in the carriage coming away from the ferry
landing, during the clandestine meeting in the art museum and,
finally, during the farewell dinner for Ellen—they reach out to
each other across aching distances. At Newport, following a long
separation, Archer has a chance to see Ellen again when his hostess
asks him to fetch her from the pier. He spots her from a distance and
stands watching her awhile. Then he turns and walks back to the
house. It is a rehearsal of the gesture he will make, some twenty years
later, in the epilogue. At such moments one may measure the force of
Edith Wharton's sudden anguished revelation to Charles du Bos, in
the year that witnessed the climax of her domestic troubles: "Ah,
the poverty, the miserable poverty, of any love that lies outside of
marriage, of any love that is not a living together, a sharing of all!"

In everything but the quality of its craftsmanship, *The Age of
Innocence* is related most clearly to the novels which followed it

rather than to those Edith Wharton wrote before the war, and chiefly because the later novels will renew the protest against innocence—the modern innocence of the Twenties. Accurately or not, Edith Wharton found the main impulse of the postwar generation in its desire to throw off every kind of restraint imposed on conduct, morals, religion—and literary expression. With no such faith in this vision of the individual, solitary and erect, bearing no taint of original sin and no past to encumber him, she found that the case she had formulated against her parents' generation was applicable to their grandchildren's. Each sought in its own way to escape the common lot; each, in its effort to avoid pain and responsibility, had weakened its moral fiber. Where convention was concerned, freedom was no better than slavery; and so Edith Wharton continued the search for a compromise on which all of her energies as a novelist were habitually bent.

Edith Wharton: A Memoir by an English Friend

by Edmund Wilson

Portrait of Edith Wharton, by Percy Lubbock, will be read with fascination by anyone interested in its subject. It is the first important memoir of the novelist that has been published since her death; and it is a literary performance of some distinction—not the usual sketch by a friend, but a real portrait, carefully composed, with every brush-stroke studied. The book is, in fact, so very much "written" that the writing sometimes has the effect of obscuring the actualities which the author is trying to describe. Mr. Lubbock, who edited Henry James's letters is one of James's most faithful disciples, and he here follows the Jamesian procedure of writing around his subject instead of showing it to us directly. He prefers to adumbrate Mrs. Wharton with metaphors or to generalize about her with abstractions rather than tell you what she said and did, how she looked and what she wore; and the result is that we seem to be gazing at her through a kind of sea mist that never clears and through which we can make out her movements and shape but are unable to scrutinize her features. It is a pleasure to read prose so well worked, in the sense that a tapestry is worked, but, like a tapestry, the book presents a series of somewhat conventionally posed tableaux—Edith Wharton just arrived in England, Edith Wharton in her household in the Faubourg Saint Germain, Edith Wharton in Morocco, and so on—which rather lack depth and detail.

The concrete questions that one would have to have answered in

order to understand Edith Wharton's career are mostly either ignored or evaded by Mr. Lubbock. Mrs. Wharton was always quite
rich. Where did her money come from? Was it her own or was it her
husband's? And why did she marry Edward Wharton, with whom
she obviously had little in common and was not very much in love?
What, precisely, was the matter with him when he became deranged
and Mrs. Wharton finally divorced him? Mr. Lubbock tries to put
their relationship in as attractive a light as possible, but then he
later speaks of Walter Berry, the American lawyer in Paris with
whom Edith Wharton's name has always been associated, as "the
man she had loved for a lifetime, in youth and age." To what kind
of situation had this given rise? There is a legend that Edith Jones's
first love was broken up by her mother, who disapproved of it and
sent her abroad; and that her first book of poems, which she had
secretly had printed, was discovered and destroyed by her family.
Is it true? And is it true that she began writing fiction, some years
after her marriage, as the result of a nervous breakdown at the
suggestion of S. Weir Mitchell, the novelist and neurologist? It has
been asserted by persons who should be in a position to know that
Edith Wharton had some reason for believing herself to have been
an illegitimate child and that her family rather let her down from
the point of view of social backing—which would account for the
curiously perfunctory, idyllic, and unreal way in which she writes of
her parents in *A Backward Glance,* as contrasted with her bitter
picture, in her novels of old New York, of the cruelty of social convention and the tyranny of the family group, as well as for her preoccupation with the miseries of extramarital love affairs and the
problems of young women who have to think about marrying for
money and position. The last of these themes, especially—exploited
so successfully in *The House of Mirth*—is difficult to account for
on the basis of Edith Wharton's being simply the well-born Miss
Jones, as is, perhaps, that insistence on her social prerogatives which
many who knew her, including Mr. Lubbock, found unnecessary
and exaggerated. Of all the conflicts of purpose and the stifled emotions that are expressed in Mrs. Wharton's books, you will find
little trace in the figure presented by Mr. Lubbock. Here she is
always seen as the hostess or the traveler *de grand luxe.* He in-
timates that her love for Berry was the source of a good deal of

unhappiness, that her perfectly appointed houses and her retinue of clever guests still left her unsatisfied, that her going to live in Europe and breaking her ties with America were a misfortune for her art and her life, and uneasily felt by her as such. But he fails to explain a career which has always appeared rather freakish. The vexed and aggrieved spirit that wrote Edith Wharton's best novels has no part in Mr. Lubbock's portrait, and the novels themselves—for reasons which Mr. Lubbock does not quite make clear—are mentioned only incidentally.

Mr. Lubbock, however, is not to be blamed. Since he was an old and intimate friend, it was probably impossible for him to go behind his subject's façade less discreetly than he has done; and the fact that he is an Englishman—he has apparently never been in the United States—makes it difficult for him to understand the background and the significance of Edith Wharton's work. What we get from him is a pretty full account of how she behaved in Europe and how she seemed to Europeans. He has added to those we already have a new picture of the literary group—which comes to seem more important as time goes on—that centered around Mrs. Wharton, Henry James, and Howard Sturgis, the Anglicized American who wrote *Belchamber*. And he has supplemented his own impressions with those of various other friends, American, English, and French, which Mr. Gaillard Lapsley, Edith Wharton's literary executor, has persuaded them to write down at length.

But the American end of the story is largely left a blank. You cannot even see the "port of New York"—it lies beyond the Atlantic and Mr. Lubbock's vision—where Edith Wharton was born, which did as much to mold her mind as Europe (it is precisely one of the functions of Manhattan to blend and to concentrate the influences of the rest of the world), and which—in her sharpness and smartness, her efficiency, her glitter and her cruelty—she so brilliantly reflected in her work. Mr. Lubbock, in his ignorance of America, has made several glaring blunders. When he comes to do a kindly little sketch of the history of American fiction up to what he calls "the uproarious Boston tea party" of the movement that came of age in the Twenties, he describes it as if it mainly consisted of or were adequately represented by Hawthorne, Howells and James—a "procession . . . united in their order for all their disparity, marching

in honor and sobriety," of which Edith Wharton brings up the rear.
Not to attempt to supply the deficiencies of Mr. Lubbock's picture,
I will point out that Mrs. Wharton was as much a contributor to
the realism of the age that followed hers as she was an inheritor
from James, and that a book like *The Custom of the Country*
opened the way for novels like *Babbitt* and *Manhattan Transfer*.
What she did that these older American writers mentioned by Mr.
Lubbock had hardly attempted at all, but that the later writers
made their chief business, was draw up a terrific indictment against
the new America of money values that, swelling to monstrous
proportions during the years after the Civil War, confronted the
world at the end of the century. Nor is it true, as Mr. Lubbock
asserts, that this later group of writers "cast overboard the wares of
the old world," whereas all the earlier ones had been "still of Europe
in their art, and in much more than their art, in the climate of their
culture, in the style and habit of their thought." Lewis, Dos Passos,
Faulkner, and Hemingway have obviously owed as much to European writers and European travel as Hawthorne and Howells had
done, and if the stories of Sherwood Anderson grew up, like the
native grass, without any foreign fertilizer, so had those of Mark
Twain, who belonged to the Howells era.

Another error of Mr. Lubbock's appears in connection with his
attitude toward Edith Wharton's heroes. We can agree with him
that many of these heroes must have been inspired by Walter Berry,
and we lack evidence to dispute his contention that Edith Wharton's
closest male friend was dry, empty-hearted and worldly, a pretentious
and unlikable snob. We certainly get the impression that Mr.
Lubbock has a grudge against Berry for encouraging Edith Wharton
in her skepticism about religion, and that he would like to believe
that, without him, she might at last have accepted the Catholic
faith. In any case, Mr. Lubbock believes that Walter Berry, to whom
Edith Wharton showed all her work and who sat in judgment on it,
was responsible for some of its faults. But he is certainly mistaken in
supposing that Mrs. Wharton idealized uncritically those of her
characters who were based on Berry. On the contrary, the male type
which most conspicuously recurs in her novels is the cultivated intelligent man who cannot bear to offend social convention, the reformer who gets bribed without knowing it in marrying a rich wife,

the family man who falls in love with someone more exciting than his wife but doesn't have the courage of his passion; and the treatment of these characters by the author, though outwardly sympathetic, is always well chilled with an irony that has an undercurrent of scorn. It is a phenomenon unfamiliar to Europe, this connoisseur whose culture is sterile, this idealist whose impulses are thwarted, this romantic who cannot act his romance, because, in every one of these roles, he is made helpless by a commercial civilization. But Edith Wharton knew him well, and she never ceased to resent him because he had failed to stand up to the temptations and threats of that civilization and because he had not been strong enough to save from that moneyed world, in which it was even easier for a woman than for a man to be caught, a woman, courageous herself, whom he might have, whom he should have, loved.

Certainly the question of money had been and always remained extremely important for Edith Wharton. Her work is the record of a struggle between wealth and its advantages, on the one hand, and aesthetic and moral values, on the other. (The fortunes of her family, Mr. Lubbock implies, was derived from New York real estate, and insofar as she was dependent on this, she must have found herself in the situation of owing her standard of living to the very extravagances of the speculative and vulgar society which she was constantly castigating.) And for this reason, if her life is to be understood, the facts about it should be brought to light. Her work, I believe, has never been—and was not, even at the time of her greatest success—appreciated or interpreted as it should be; and it is possible that her personal history, which now appears merely puzzling, would provide a dramatic illustration of the tragedy often incurred and the heroism sometimes engendered by a period of American life which imposed upon human beings peculiar and extreme conditions. The papers of Edith Wharton now deposited in the Yale University Library are not, I understand, to be published before 1968, but we may hope to have eventually a biography that will tell the whole of her story and show her in her full dimensions.

Chronology of Important Dates

1862	Born, in New York City, to George and Lucretia Jones
1878	Privately publishes juvenile *Verses*
1885	Marries Edward Wharton
1889	Publishes first poems in *Scribner's Magazine*
1897	Publishes *The Decoration of Houses* together with Ogden Codman
1899	Publishes first book of stories, *The Greater Inclination*
1902	Publishes first novel, *The Valley of Decision*
1902	Begins friendship with Henry James
1905	Publishes *The House of Mirth*
1907	Settles in Paris
1908	Edward Wharton suffers nervous breakdown
1911	Publishes *Ethan Frome*
1913	Divorced from Edward Wharton
1913	Publishes *The Custom of the Country*
1914-1918	Devotes herself to hospital and charity work in wartime France
1917	Publishes *Summer*
1920	Awarded Pulitzer Prize for *The Age of Innocence*
1923	Receives from Yale University honorary award of Doctor of Letters
1930	Elected to the American Academy of Arts and Letters
1937	Dies in France

Notes on the Editor and Authors

IRVING HOWE, Professor of English at Stanford University, is a literary critic and political writer. He is editor of *Dissent*, contributing editor of *The New Republic*, and author of a number of books, among them *Politics and the Novel, William Faulkner: A Critical Study,* and *Sherwood Anderson: A Critical Biography*.

LOUIS AUCHINCLOSS is the author of a collection of literary essays, *Reflections of a Jacobite*, and several novels.

The late E. K. BROWN was Professor of English at the University of Rochester, author of a critical study of Willa Cather and *Edith Wharton: Étude Critique*.

LOUIS O. COXE teaches at Bowdoin College and is a poet and the author of a dramatic version of *Billy Budd*.

HENRY JAMES, the great American novelist, was a friend of Mrs. Wharton.

ALFRED KAZIN, an influential literary critic, has written *On Native Grounds, A Walker in the City, Contemporaries,* and other books.

Q. D. LEAVIS, is the author of *Fiction and the Reading Public*, and has contributed a number of essays to the critical journal *Scrutiny*.

The late PERCY LUBBOCK, author of *The Craft of Fiction* and *Portrait of Edith Wharton*, was a close friend of Mrs. Wharton.

BLAKE NEVIUS, who teaches at the University of California at Los Angeles, is the author of *Edith Wharton*, a full-length critical study.

V. L. PARRINGTON was, before his death, Professor of English at the University of Washington. He is the author of the well-known study of American intellectual history, *Main Currents of American Thought*.

DIANA TRILLING is a literary and political writer who has contributed to *Partisan Review, The Nation*, and other magazines.

LIONEL TRILLING, Professor of English at Columbia University, is well-known for his essays, collected under the titles *The Liberal Imagination* and *The Opposing Self*.

EDMUND WILSON, perhaps the most distinguished American critic of our time, has written *Axel's Castle, The Wound and the Bow, The Triple Thinkers,* and many other books.

Bibliography of the Major Writings of Edith Wharton

Verses. Newport: C. E. Hammett, Jr., 1878.
The Decoration of Houses (with Ogden Codman, Jr.). New York: Scribner's, 1897.
The Greater Inclination. New York: Scribner's, 1899.
The Touchstone. New York: Scribner's, 1900. Published in England as *A Gift from the Grave* (London: John Murray, 1900).
Crucial Instances. New York: Scribner's, 1901.
The Valley of Decision. New York: Scribner's, 1902. 2 vols.
Sanctuary. New York: Scribner's, 1903.
The Descent of Man, and Other Stories. New York: Scribner's, 1904.
Italian Villas and Their Gardens. New York: Century, 1904.
Italian Backgrounds. New York: Scribner's, 1905.
The House of Mirth. New York: Scribner's, 1905.
Madame de Treymes. New York: Scribner's, 1907.
The Fruit of the Tree. New York: Scribner's, 1907.
A Motor-Flight through France. New York: Scribner's, 1908.
The Hermit and the Wild Woman and Other Stories. New York: Scribner's, 1908.
Artemis to Actaeon and Other Verse. New York: Scribner's, 1909.
Tales of Men and Ghosts. New York: Scribner's, 1910.
Ethan Frome. New York: Scribner's, 1911.
The Reef. New York: Appleton, 1912.
The Custom of the Country. New York: Scribner's, 1913.
Fighting France, from Dunkerque to Belfort. New York: Scribner's, 1915.
Xingu and Other Stories. New York: Scribner's, 1916.
Summer. New York: Appleton, 1917.
The Marne. New York: Appleton, 1918.
French Ways and Their Meaning. New York: Appleton, 1919.
The Age of Innocence. New York: Appleton, 1920.
In Morocco. New York: Scribner's, 1920.
The Glimpses of the Moon. New York: Appleton, 1922.
A Son at the Front. New York: Scribner's, 1923.
Old New York: False Dawn (The Forties); *The Old Maid* (The Fifties); *The Spark* (The Sixties); *New Year's Day* (The Seventies). New York: Appleton, 1924. 4 vols.

The Mother's Recompense. New York: Appleton, 1925.
The Writing of Fiction. New York: Scribner's, 1925.
Here and Beyond. New York: Appleton, 1926.
Twelve Poems. London: The Medici Society, 1926.
Twilight Sleep. New York: Appleton, 1927.
The Children. New York: Appleton, 1928.
Hudson River Bracketed. New York: Appleton, 1929.
Certain People. New York: Appleton, 1930.
The Gods Arrive. New York: Appleton, 1932.
Human Nature. New York: Appleton, 1933.
A Backward Glance. New York: Appleton-Century, 1934.
The World Over. New York: Appleton-Century, 1936.
Ghosts. New York: Appleton-Century, 1937.
The Buccaneers. New York: Appleton-Century, 1938.

Selected Bibliography on Edith Wharton

The amount of first-rate critical writing about Mrs. Wharton is limited; much of it appears in this volume.

Mrs. Wharton's autobiographical volume, *A Backward Glance* (New York: Appleton-Century-Crofts, 1934), is extremely reticent concerning the facts of her life but nevertheless valuable as a revelation of her outlook and bias. Percy Lubbock's *Portrait of Edith Wharton* (New York: Appleton-Century-Crofts, 1947), is a fascinating compendium of miniature essays, letters, and comments by Mrs. Wharton's friends, all of which are bound together by Lubbock's astute observations. Important biographical material, including excerpts from Mrs. Wharton's journals, appears in Wayne Andrews' Introduction to *The Best Short Stories of Edith Wharton*, (New York: Scribner's, 1958). There is no full-scale biography available and, until Mrs. Wharton's papers at Yale University are opened in 1968, none can be written.

Among the critical studies of Mrs. Wharton's work, the only one that can be recommended without serious reservations is Blake Nevius' careful book, *Edith Wharton* (Berkeley: U. of California Press, 1953). There are critical comments, of varying outlook and uneven value, in Joseph Warren Beach's *The Twentieth Century Novel: Studies in Technique* (New York: Appleton-Century-Crofts, 1932); Frederick Hoffman's *The Modern Novel in America: 1900-1950* (New York: Regnery, 1951); Van Wyck Brooks's *The Confident Years* (New York: Dutton, 1952); Henry James's *Notes on Novelists* (New York: Scribner's, 1914); Robert Morss Lovett's *Edith Wharton* (New York: McBride, 1925); Katherine Mansfield's *Novels and Novelists* (New York: Knopf, 1930); Stuart Sherman's *The Main Stream* (New York: Scribner's, 1927).

Two essays which, in addition to those in the present volume, might be helpful to the reader and student of Mrs. Wharton's novels, are Frederick Hoffman, "Points of Moral Reference: A Comparative Study of Edith Wharton and F. Scott Fitzgerald," *English Institute Essays* (New York: Columbia U. Press, 1949), and John Crowe Ransom, "Characters and Character," *American Review*, January 1936.

TWENTIETH CENTURY VIEWS

Forthcoming Titles